BISMARCK
and German Unification

IMMORTALS OF HISTORY

BISMARCK

and German Unification

Louis L. Snyder
and
Ida Mae Brown

Franklin Watts, Inc.
575 Lexington Avenue
New York, N.Y. 10022

Contents

v

CONTENTS

To the memory of
Rosa Brown

He was the son of a soldier and country gentleman, and was very proud of his origin, especially of the fact that his ancestors had fought in all the great Prussian wars. Bismarck always retained the tastes, although he lost some of the prejudices, of his class. He was fond of good fare, ate and drank largely, and was devoted to the chase. He was a master of pithy, vigorous, and homely speech, and believed in the use of force. He had by nature a contempt for anything weak.

He had the most powerful brain of his time; but like all very great men, he depended for his strength upon a few simple, clear ideas. He was determined to make Prussia great, and he was convinced that Prussia could only exist if certain social and religious habits and institutions were untouched.

He could be passionate and ruthless. He was brutal in the exercise of his determination, and would lie awake at night indulging in the luxury of hatred. He had few friends, and formed no very intimate relations outside those of his family and his dogs.

He found himself slowly. As a student he lived fast; as a young politician he was suspected, in spite of his courage, as passionate and eccentric; even as minister he was, for some time, lightly esteemed as the incompetent head of a reactionary set. But when his energy once found expression and fell under the control of his mind, he was irresistible. In his old age, his brain was "like a printing press, working incessantly, without any paper to print upon."

There is no historical parallel to Bismarck.

—*Condensed from F. M. Powicke,* Bismarck and the Origins of the German Empire (*London, 1914*), *pp. 10–13. Courtesy of T. C. and E. C. Jack.*

CHAPTER ONE

Otto von Bismarck:
Immortal of History

*"Not by parliamentary majorities are the
great questions of the day settled—that was
the great blunder of 1848 and 1849—but by
iron and blood."*

He was like some great Pharaoh hewn from Egyptian
rock. His physical qualities alone gave him titanic
force. Powerfully built, he carried his body with military stiffness in movements that were bold and dignified. His head was large (after his death his brain was
found to be larger in size than any other man of his
day). The face was unforgettable. Over the arched
forehead were a few strands of blond hair. The mus-
tache was thick. The bulging eyes were clear and
lively. The complexion, fixed by bodily suffering, was
pale.

This was Otto Eduard Leopold von Bismarck-Schön-

1

hausen, known to the whole world as Bismarck. This was the born leader of men—the horseman, hunter, forester, and guide of his people in war and peace. The greatest German since Martin Luther, Bismarck was in truth an immortal. Not only was he the most important man in the history of Germany, but also of the entire European continent in the second half of the nineteenth century.

The work of Bismarck had greater effect than that of any other statesman or diplomat of his time. He was the man who fashioned the unity of Germany in the heart of Europe. He led wars against Denmark in 1864, against Austria in 1866, and against France in 1870–1871. From 1871 until his resignation in 1890, he brought Prussia-Germany to greatness and at the same time maintained the peace of Europe. He also contributed much to the spirit and mentality of the German people.

Bismarck was the man of "blood and iron." It was a phrase he coined, and he was never able to free himself from the reputation that went along with it. No statesman of his day came up to his level—he succeeded in outwitting them all. Governmental leaders recognized Bismarck's superiority as a diplomat. Jules Favre, the French foreign minister, who had the unenviable task of negotiating peace with Bismarck in 1871, called him "a statesman who surpasses everything one can imagine."

Together with the towering physical body went a great intellect. Bismarck was a man of immense insight. He was able to drive at once to the heart of any problem. It was this ability which enabled him to outwit his political opponents at home and his enemies abroad. Added to this quality was a truly phenomenal breadth of vision. He had a rare capacity to anticipate the future and, therefore, to act in the best interests of his country. A master of intrigue and strategy, he would often confuse his opponents by merely telling the truth.

A man of tremendous courage, he repeatedly revealed his fearlessness—especially in his boyhood days, when he led his friends in mimic battles. He showed his bravery in student duels, and also when one day he plunged into deep water to rescue his drowning groom. Throughout his life he exhibited this same lack of fear, as once, when unarmed, he grappled with a would-be assassin.

He had great loves and great hates. He loved his wife and family, and he hated his political enemies. He was a man of caustic wit and humor. In both his letters and table talk, one finds many examples of flowing humor, funny remarks, and practical jokes. At the same time he displayed a sincerity which came from a deep sense of duty.

He was a man of enormous appetite. He performed extraordinary feats at the table where he was inclined

3

to hold his own against all comers. He was fond of plovers' eggs and usually consumed fifteen at one meal. On one occasion he astonished the waiters of a restaurant when he ate one hundred and seventy oysters. He loved beer and wines, of which he consumed many thousands of bottles. For all this, however, he paid a heavy penalty. During the later years of his life he suffered from crippling neuralgic pains in the face. Sometimes he could hardly open his mouth. This was quite natural, he said in jest, because he had sinned mostly with his mouth—in eating, drinking, and speaking.

This was the many-sided personality of Germany's great Chancellor. His was a fascinating life, filled with action, with joys and sorrow, with victory and defeat.

CHAPTER TWO

Birth, Parentage, and Early Life

"I was miserable at boarding school."

> I have the honor to announce to
> my friends that yesterday my wife
> was safely delivered of a son, and
> I excuse them from offering con-
> gratulations.
>
> —Ferdinand von Bismarck
>
> Schönhausen
> 2nd of April 1815

This highly unusual notice, placed in the *Vossische
Zeitung,* announced the birth on April 1, 1815, of Otto
von Bismarck at the manor house of Schönhausen in
the Mark (boundary-state) of Brandenburg. The

child's father, Ferdinand von Bismarck, only twenty-four years old, had left the army the year before in order to devote his life to managing the estate which he had inherited. Little is known about him, except that he had only a limited influence on the formation of his son's character.

Ferdinand von Bismarck was a Prussian "Junker," that curious class of aristocratic, Teutonic origin which had been sent to northeast Germany to win and hold the land from the western Slavs. In the east Elbian area arose a hard-riding, hard-drinking, hard-fighting lesser nobility. These Junkers were loyal first to themselves and secondly to the royal Hohenzollern family. They were a selfish, obstinate, arrogant, wooden-headed crowd. To indicate their noble origin they proudly used *von* in their names. From this Junker class came most of the officers and officials of Prussia. They regarded themselves as a superior lot—as colonists on conquered soil. The peasants of the area became accustomed to bowing low before their Junker superiors. Young Otto von Bismarck belonged to this class. "I am a Junker," he said, "and mean to profit from it."

Otto could boast of nobility only on his father's side. Ferdinand von Bismarck might have married one of his own rank, but instead he took as his wife the sixteen-year-old Fräulein Wilhelmine Mencken whose family had produced a long line of professors of law

6

and state administrators. A shrewd, ambitious woman, she was more mentally alert than her mediocre husband. Thus Otto was influenced by two Prussian traits: on his father's side he was descended from fighting nobles; on his mother's side from scholars and officials. From his father he absorbed geniality and humor; from his mother sensitive nerves, zest for living, and keen intelligence. Yet, he never really appreciated his mother. Rather, he resented her hard discipline, and believed that she was lacking in motherly love. Besides, she always seemed to be making him do things he did not want to do.

Otto did not live at Schönhausen very long. When he was only a year old, he was taken by his parents northward to the province of Pomerania to another family estate called Kniephof. Here, too, the Prussian nobility held to the feudal way of life, with medieval beliefs and loyalty for the monarchy. As their fathers had before them, the Junkers were ready at an instant to draw their swords and defend the king against foreigners, liberals, and atheists.

Wilhelmine Mencken was ambitious for her son. She not only decided that he would become a diplomat, but she also believed strong discipline would be best for young Otto. Instead of engaging a tutor, as was the custom then among Junker families, she sent him away from his happy surroundings to a boarding

7

school when he was only seven years old. Her reason, she said, was "to break his aristocratic pride." The sensitive boy never forgave his mother for that.

Otto went to Plamann's Institute in Berlin, which was noted for its harsh curriculum. The school was run along the lines suggested by the eccentric patriot, Turnvater Jahn. Under the Jahn method the boys got little to eat, were exposed to rough training, and had to build up their bodies by hard exercise. Every morning they were awakened promptly at six o'clock and given a breakfast of milk and bread. After religious exercises, they began their lessons at seven. At noon came dinner. Each boy, on pain of punishment, had to eat every bit of food on his plate. Lessons continued from two to four. Then tea-time followed. After seven, games were allowed until supper which consisted of warm beer and several slices of bread.

Otto hated the school. He complained bitterly of the masters because they insisted on tough gymnastics and athletic games which he loathed. He was so homesick for the carefree life of the country that, when out walking one day, he burst into tears upon seeing a plow. It reminded him of home. The other boys, uniting against the newcomer, decided to haze him. They hatched a plot to duck him in a nearby stream. But Otto, aware of their scheme, plunged into the water, swam under the surface, and came up on the opposite bank. From that moment, his comrades, who were delighted by his daring, accepted him as an equal. He soon became their leader in war games and was elected captain of the snowball team.

After five years at Plamann's boarding school, Otto, now at the beginning of his thirteenth year, was transferred to the Friedrich Wilhelm Gymnasium (high school) in Berlin. He immediately attracted the attention of one of the masters, Professor Bonnell, who later wrote:

My eyes were drawn to Bismarck on the very day of his entry, on which occasion the new boys sat in the school room on rows of benches in order that the masters could watch the newcomers during the inauguration proceedings. Otto von Bismarck sat—as I still distinctly remember—with visible eagerness, a clear and pleasant boyish face and bright eyes, in a gay and lightsome mood among his comrades. I said to myself: "That's a bright boy. I'll have to keep an eye on him."

Young Otto was one of the very best pupils in the school. He showed such powers of understanding and his talents were so great that he was able to do his work without much exertion. He especially liked the study of history, which became for him a lifelong passion. He got into many disputes with his French professor, whom he detested. He knew that he could

9

avoid tests given by this teacher because he was allowed to choose either English or French for his final essay. He chose English, which he learned in an incredibly short time.

In 1830, at the age of fifteen, Bismarck was confirmed in Berlin by the celebrated theologian and philosopher, Friedrich Schleiermacher. The old man cautioned him: "Whatever you do, do it for God, and not for men." At this time Otto left the Gymnasium and was sent to another school called the Grey Cloisters.

In 1831, when the school term was nearly ended, the dread disease of cholera broke out in the big cities of eastern Europe. People were paralyzed by fear as they saw the epidemic sweeping nearer and nearer to them. Otto's father, concerned about his son, wrote to him that at the first outbreak of cholera in Berlin he was to start at once for Kniephof. Otto became wildly excited because this meant a chance to return to his home. He hired a swift horse and galloped to the eastern gate of Berlin, from which district the cholera was expected. He wanted to see for himself whether or not the disease was approaching the city.

The adventure ended in sudden disaster when Otto's horse stumbled and fell on top of him. Otto was picked up with a crushed leg and sent back to school in a hansom cab. To his annoyance he had to remain in bed while convalescing. He soon recovered, but it was too late to go home, for cholera had come to Berlin.

Some weeks later he was able to leave the capital for his beloved country home.

At Easter, 1832, Otto's school days came to an end. He had studied very seriously and had learned the essentials of reading, writing, and arithmetic. He passed with honors the final Gymnasium examination, called the *Abitur*. He submitted a prize essay in Latin, but, curiously, the judgment on it was: *"Oratio est lucida ac latina, sed non satis castigata"* ("The language is clear and Latin-like, but not sufficiently polished").

When he was graduated from the Gymnasium, Otto was seventeen years of age, tall and slender, "thin as a knitting needle." His face was pale but his health was good. He was a hearty eater. Although occasionally shy, he was generally outgoing and had a frank and free manner about him. His favorite pastimes were riding and hunting. He swam well, was a good fencer and dancer, but was annoyed by organized sports. He loved animals, especially horses and dogs. He owned a Danish dog, which became a familiar sight around the neighborhood of Kniephof.

Otto von Bismarck was an active, joyful teenager. Few people guessed at this time that he would become one of the greatest immortals of German history.

CHAPTER THREE

A Hell Raiser at Göttingen and Berlin

*"The bottle probably flew out of
the window by itself."*

When the time came for him to attend a university,
Bismarck wanted to go to Heidelberg. But his mother
objected. She had heard stories about too much beer
drinking by students there. Instead, she chose the University of Göttingen, which had a good reputation for
the teaching of law and history. Otto, who longed for
the joys of academic freedom, agreed to this change.

At the start of his university career, Bismarck did
not have the remotest idea of the nature of student life.
But he soon learned and even proceeded to set his
own rules. Moreover, he decided to make up for the
miserable days he had suffered as a schoolboy. His
wild rebellion took the form of striking out at everyone
and at everything that disturbed him.

12

Göttingen University never saw anyone like young Bismarck. He became the most notorious hell raiser in the history of that venerable institution. A nonconformist, he wanted to be different, to be above the mob of students, to do exactly what he wished without anyone giving him orders.

The people of the town of Göttingen were amused to see the explosive young Junker moving through the narrow streets of their old town. He wore an ostentatious velvet dressing gown, an outlandish cap, and carried a twisted iron staff in his hand. He was followed obediently by a wobbly little *Dachshund* with a flower tied to its tail. If any student dared to laugh, he would be challenged to a duel. "I can protect myself against insults," Bismarck would say, "but my little dog Fritz cannot. If you don't get down on your knees and apologize to him by barking in a language he understands, you will have to fight me."

From the beginning of his university career Bismarck showed little interest in learning. He was lazier than the average student. Bored by the lectures given by his professors, he was convinced that he knew more than they did. Soon he stopped attending classes altogether. With his good brain and retentive memory he read only what interested him.

Because he knew English, he was able to make acquaintances with young Englishmen and Americans who had been attracted to Göttingen by its great reputation. He formed a lifetime friendship with an American named John Lothrop Motley, who later became a famous historian and American ambassador to Austria and later to England. Motley was one of the few human beings ever to enjoy Bismarck's genuine affection.

Bismarck's mother was not very successful in keeping him away from beer. He soon became a champion at the student beer-drinking bouts called *Kneiperei*. In order to sober up, he would often return to his little room, which was alongside a stream and, without hesitation, hurl himself out of the window into the water.

One evening Bismarck gave a party for some fellow students at the Golden Crown Hotel. They drank great quantities of beer and wine, and no one noticed an empty bottle being thrown out of the window. A passing policeman reported the incident.

The next morning Bismarck sat at his window nursing a hangover. Someone tapped at his door. It was a university officer called a *beadle*, who held a piece of paper in his hand. Bismarck knew instantly what it was—an order calling him to the dean's office. He went along, wearing his gay dressing gown and slippers, and accompanied at his heel by a huge, whitish-yellow hound.

The dean, in his study, was astonished and badly frightened when Bismarck's dog bounded straight for him. The old man retreated behind a barricade of chairs to evade the big animal.

"What do you want?" he asked Bismarck.

"Me? I want nothing," was the reply. "It is you who want something, since you were the one who sent me this summons."

The dean, whose bearing had been anything but dignified, began to recover his confidence.

"Sir," he said sternly, "in the first place I order you to pay a fine of five thalers for having brought that animal here. Secondly, I want you to explain how that bottle came to be thrown out of the window of the Golden Crown last evening. I have the pieces of that bottle here."

"*Mein Gott*, sir! The bottle probably flew out of the window by itself!"

"That is silly," said the dean. "How can a bottle fly by itself? Someone must have thrown it!"

"Perhaps so, sir!"

"Perhaps, nothing! Please be more explicit."

"Well, it probably happened this way." Bismarck seized a large ink stand on the desk and pretended to throw it at the dean's head.

The dean had had enough. Perhaps this crazy student would really throw the ink stand.

"*Heraus!*" he shrieked, pointing to the door. "Get out!"

It is not recorded that Bismarck ever did pay the fine.

During his second half-year semester at Göttingen, Bismarck was summoned to appear before the university's academic tribunal. He was accused of having taken part in a duel with pistols. He gave this evidence:

Quite by accident I entered into the Gurkenkrug Brewery, and I found there some fellow students who were in a quandary. A duel with pistols had been arranged, and the person chosen for umpire had not arrived. My comrades urged me to take his place, and I consented. I did all I could to induce the young men to make it up, but in vain. So I insisted on the condition that the two adversaries should fire at ten paces, and not over a handkerchief as had at first been agreed upon. My proposal having been accepted, I measured the distance, counting twelve paces. And when you consider the length of my legs, you will see, gentlemen, that my intention was to render the duel less dangerous. But this was not all: I stipulated that only just enough powder should be put into the pistols to force out the bullets. I think, then, I have some reason to believe that all the merits of the harmless issue of this duel belong to me.

16

According to the university archives, Bismarck's ingenious explanation did not meet with the approval of the authorities. He was condemned to three days' confinement in the "Black Hole," a special prison cell for student offenders. Even today, visitors can see Bismarck's name which he carved on the wooden door of his cell.

More common than the pistol duels, however, were the student duels with swords. These were called the *Mensuren*. They were traditional in the German states of those days, and were even considered to be a good form of sport. Such contests were supposed to be a test of German courage. To be cut on the face was regarded as a great honor. Students wore their dueling scars proudly for the rest of their lives.

The form and procedures of the *Mensuren* were carefully regulated by tradition. One student would walk up to another and say: *"Guten Tag, du dummer Junge, du!"* ("Good day, you stupid fellow!") The other would reply: "And good day to *you*, you fool!" Then the two would exchange cards and arrange for a duel. A *Fuchs* (fox, or freshman) had to fight a certain number of duels before he was eligible to wear the cap and colors of his fraternity.

On the day of combat the duelists were clothed in padded material covering hands, arms, chest, and neck, but not the face. They stood flat-footed facing each other as the swords flashed down from above. To step back one inch or blink an eye was considered to be cowardly. The duel consisted of a number of rounds (*Gänge*) of about a minute each. The proceedings were watched by a *Pauk-Doktor* (dueling doctor), usually an old-time medical student who could never get his degree. The winner was the one who first slashed his opponent across the face, whereupon the action was instantly stopped.

Foreigners described the duels as barbarous. But to German students they were wonderful sport. "The worst that can happen," went one remark, "is to get a nose or ear chopped off, and they can always be sewed back on again."

The whole idea of dueling appealed to young Bismarck. Whenever he issued a challenge, he would always add: "And when I say 'Stupid fellow!' I really mean it!" He was seen more often in the fencing rooms than in the lecture halls. He soon had a reputation as the best swordsman on the campus. At Göttingen, Bismarck fought twenty-seven duels, of which he won twenty-six. He was wounded only once, when his adversary's blade broke and cut his face. For the rest of his life he was proud of that scar, a visible symbol of his fearlessness.

I In September of 1833, after spending a little more than a year at Göttingen, Bismarck applied for permission to transfer to the University of Berlin.*I* It was granted on condition that he serve a term of imprisonment which he owed the Göttingen authorities. Yet it is not known whether he served this term or not.

Bismarck spent the next three semesters at Berlin University. Once again he found student life far too enjoyable to mend his ways. "I devoted myself again to my old mistress, the bottle." On some evenings he went to the opera, where he behaved as boorishly as possible. Sometimes he would join a bull session with Motley and a German friend named Keyserling, with whom he sang his favorite American song: "In Good Old Colony Times":

> *In good old colony times,*
> *When we lived under a king,*
> *Three roguish chaps*
> *Fell into mishaps*
> *Because they could not sing. . . .*

❘ Then came the specter of final examinations. Bismarck summoned all his will power and for the first time went to several lectures, including those of the great law professor, Savigny. In the short period remaining he engaged the services of a "crammer," which was a customary procedure at the time. With the assistance of this coach, Bismarck managed to learn enough to pass his examinations. His strength of intellect made up for his lack of attendance in the lecture halls.❘

CHAPTER FOUR

The Mad Junker

"I will play music as I like it, or none at all."

For a young Prussian nobleman of Bismarck's background there were only two possible careers: he could become an officer in the Prussian army, or he could go into government service. Bismarck was not attracted by the military life because of its strict discipline. Furthermore, he disliked anyone telling him what to do. He decided on government service.

In 1835, again with the help of a crammer, Bismarck passed his examinations for administrative work. His first appointment was as *Auskultator* (examiner) in the judicial department in Berlin. The story is told of how he questioned a Berliner who was brought before the police court as a witness. Bismarck was so annoyed by the responses of the man that he jumped up from his seat and cried: "Sir, behave better, or I'll have you kicked out!"

The magistrate patted Bismarck on the shoulder in a friendly way and said quietly: *"Herr Auskultator,* the kicking out is *my* business."

The trial went on and more evidence was taken. But once again Bismarck sprang to his feet and thundered at the witness: "Sir, you'd better behave yourself, or the magistrate will kick you out!"

After a year in this unpaid work, Bismarck passed another legal examination as *Referendar,* or junior lawyer. At his own request he was transferred to Aix-la-Chapelle (present-day Aachen). The choice was probably due to the fact that the president of the province in which Aix-la-Chapelle is located was Count Arnim von Boytzenburg, a relative of the Bismarck family. Here, in the famous summer resort town, which was a meeting place for international society, Bismarck was supposed to learn all about administrative and judicial work.

But the explosive young Junker had little taste for hard work. He preferred to spend his time in the more agreeable pursuits of drinking or playing at gaming tables, where he consistently lost. He liked the company of wealthy Englishmen who were traveling on the Continent. Through them he met a beautiful girl named Laura Russell, but nothing came of the romance. A few months later he again fell in love with another English girl, Isabella Lorraine. For her, Bismarck left his post. He followed her through central

Europe, only to lose her to "a fifty-year-old colonel with one arm, four horses, and a 15,000-thaler-a-year income."

In June, 1837, Bismarck applied for a leave of absence because of ill health. He was given an eight-day vacation—which he extended to four months. Trying to win at the gaming tables, he lost 17,000 thalers instead. In November, 1837, he returned penniless to Kniephof, and resolved to become a farmer. When his parents urged him to try government service again, he worked for a short time as a *Referendar* at Potsdam. But it was hopeless. He was lazy and uninterested and he finally gave it up.

Because he had not yet fulfilled the military obligation required of every young Prussian, he now began a year of active duty as a private in the *Jaeger,* or Rifles, in the *Garde Corps* stationed at Potsdam. A few weeks later he was transferred to the *Jaeger* at Stettin.

In 1839, at the age of twenty-four, Bismarck settled down with his brother, Bernhard, to the life of a country squire managing the family estate at Kniephof. Otto lived there for the next four years. He did not give up the habits he had formed as a student. If anything, he became even wilder. Thoroughly bored by the life around him, he sought escape in drinking and roistering. His own concoction, a mixture of beer and champagne, became a popular drink in the neighborhood. He would ride his horse at breakneck speed through the countryside. His idea of companionship was to awaken his friends by firing shots through their windows as they slept. It was little wonder, therefore, that this arrogant, noisy, restless, and reckless young man became known as "the wild Bismarck" and "the mad Junker."

In 1841, when he was twenty-six, Bismarck was made a lieutenant in the *Landwehr,* which was a kind of National Guard in Prussia. The next year he was called for military maneuvers with his regiment of Pomeranian Uhlans (lancers).

On the afternoon of June 24, 1842, Bismarck, accompanied by another young officer and their two servants, went for a ride on horseback. Arriving at a lake, the two officers dismounted and stood on a bridge while Bismarck's servant, Hildebrandt, and an Uhlan named Kuhl rode the horses into the water. Hildebrandt began to have trouble with his horse. Instead of going straight out from the shore, the frightened animal tried to turn around. Hildebrandt struggled with the reins, but he was thrown into deep water. Kuhl, trying to help him, also plunged into the water.

Instantly Bismarck, who was watching from the bridge, took off his tunic and jumped into the water. First he helped the sinking Uhlan to the shore and then swam out to his exhausted servant. He brought the half-drowned man to the shore. Then he went back into the water and led the horses to safety. His quick

23

thinking and action had saved the lives of two men.

Now and then Bismarck tried to get away from the boredom of life at Kniephof. From July to October, 1842, he disappeared from his haunts and journeyed to England, Scotland, France, Switzerland, and Italy. The next year brought an important turning point in the young man's life. He met Marie von Thadden, the beautiful daughter of a neighboring Pomeranian nobleman. She became the passion of his life. Of strongly pious background, Marie tried to change Bismarck from a freethinker to a good Christian—a most difficult task, indeed. Unfortunately for Bismarck, she married another man and died within a year, the victim of brain inflammation. Bismarck was shattered. He never forgot the girl he had loved.

❡ Through Marie von Thadden, Bismarck met Fräulein Johanna von Puttkamer, also of a quiet and religious family. His proposal of marriage shocked and dismayed her parents, who wanted nothing to do with the "mad Junker." But Bismarck overcame all objections and won the consent of Johanna's father. He wrote a letter in which he expressed the most pious of sentiments, saying that he had won his battle for belief in a personal God and was now entitled to ask for Johanna's hand in marriage. Admittedly, he had ceased to pray since the age of seventeen but, as Marie von Thadden lay near death, he wrote in the letter, "fervent prayer had burst forth from my heart. I have never again lost the ability to petition to Him."

It was a wonderfully clever letter. Bismarck was really sincere. For the rest of his life he remained a religious man. This letter reveals a rare understanding which was to characterize his later career. At the same time it was diplomatically shrewd. The reformed freethinker and hard gambler had won the hand of the girl of his choice.

The marriage of the tamed Junker and the pious young Johanna took place in late June, 1847. Surprisingly, it turned out to be a long and happy union.

Meanwhile Bismarck had started on his political career. In 1845 he was elected one of the members of the Provincial Diet of Pomerania. Just before his marriage he went to Berlin as a representative of the lower nobility to the United Diet, the first Prussian Parliament. From this time on the story of Bismarck's life is interwoven with the history of Prussia-Germany.

CHAPTER FIVE

Preparation: The Drive to Power, 1848–1862

"I am a Junker and I mean to profit from it."

There was no real Germany at this time. Bismarck himself was a subject of Prussia, and Prussia was only one of the hodgepodge of many German states. The medieval German emperors had never succeeded in uniting these quarreling states. Whatever German unity there was had been destroyed in the Reformation, when Catholic and Protestant states split apart. In 1815, after the fall of Napoleon I, the statesmen at the famous Congress of Vienna, in remaking the map of Europe, tried to reorganize the divided Germanies into something resembling a national state. In this task they failed.

/ When Bismarck appeared on the scene as a Prussian statesman, the German states were organized in a German Confederation (*Bund*), which was centered at

Frankfurt-am-Main and controlled by Austria. In the *Bund* were thirty-nine states, including Prussia, the kingdoms of Saxony, Hanover, Bavaria, and Württemberg, and a collection of smaller principalities. There was no German army, no German law. Every German state tried to go its separate way.

Frederick William IV (1795–1861), of the Hohenzollern dynasty, ascended the throne of Prussia in 1840. He strongly opposed a formal, written constitution for his people—although the people wanted it. On February 3, 1847, he summoned the first United Diet in Prussia. Bismarck, a delegate to this parliament, soon distinguished himself as an apostle of reaction. He was highly conservative in his ideas and took a stand opposed to democracy and liberalism. He spoke before the Diet in a most offensive manner and soon incurred disfavor among his colleagues as well as with the general public, both of whom regarded him as medieval in his views. But, for the monarchy, the court party, and the Junkers, he was the man to watch.

After their honeymoon in Venice, Bismarck and his bride went to Schönhausen to settle down to what they believed to be a quiet country life. They were mistaken. Political storms were gathering over Europe and the Bismarcks were to be carried away by them in the next forty-three years.

The revolution which began in Paris in February of 1848 drove the French king, Louis-Philippe, from the

27

throne. France now became a republic. The revolutionary wave soon spread to the Germanies. On March 18, 1848, riots broke out in Berlin with fierce fights between the people and the soldiers. The revolutionists, like those in France, called for a free, united Germany; they demanded freedom of speech, press, and assembly; they wanted a constitution. The Prussian king, virtually a prisoner in his castle, had to promise to grant a constitution. Berlin was in a reign of terror. The National Guard was unable to maintain order. Well-dressed people were afraid to appear on the streets. It seemed that the monarchy would be overthrown at any minute.

To Bismarck all this was dangerous nonsense. The news from Berlin made him ill with gall and anger. He decided to do something about it. He gathered his Schönhausen peasants, armed them with scythes and knives, and set off to the capital city. Like a belligerent medieval knight, he would save his precious king from the mob.

It was a useless gesture, but it revealed Bismarck's reckless courage when faced with an emergency. He scarcely understood the revolution: to him it was little more than a street revolt that could be put down by a counterrevolution. As for liberty, equality, and fraternity, democracy and constitutions—to Bismarck all that was French foolishness.

While he supported the Hohenzollern monarchy,

Bismarck was still inclined to blame King Frederick William IV for the revolt. The king, he said, was too weak and by his weakness had virtually invited the insurrection. "The Crown itself," he said, "has thrown the earth on its coffin." When the queen defended her husband by saying that he had not been able to sleep a minute during the awful March days, Bismarck coldly replied: "A king *must* be able to sleep."

The revolution in the Germanies soon lost its momentum. The Frankfurt Assembly, a "parliament of professors," was full of the high ideals of democracy and liberalism but, despite all the fine speeches, it collapsed. Bismarck was glad of this—he wanted no "organized anarchy." Fully aware of the political tendencies of his era, he knew that the days of absolutism were over and that the people had to have a constitution and representation. But as a conservative he wanted to preserve as much of the royal power as possible. The government of Prussia, he believed, had to be dependent on the king, not on a parliamentary majority. The king ruled by divine right—he had been sent by God to reign over the Prussian people. And at his right hand was the great noble class of Junkers, aristocrats who were born to play a leading role in Prussian life.

These were Bismarck's aims, and he meant to carry them out, with or without the wishes of the people. Let the people call him "that medieval Junker" and "that hopeless reactionary." The important things were:

(1) to retain the Prussian monarchy, and (2) to maintain the power of the Prussian Junker class.

On May 11, 1851, at the age of thirty-six, Bismarck arrived in Frankfurt-am-Main as the Prussian envoy to the German *Bund* at Frankfurt. This is an important date in German history. On that day Bismarck brought with him the will and the potential power to drive Austria out of German affairs. He was furiously opposed to the German Confederation, which was run by Austria and which was designed to keep Prussia in an inferior position.

A few months earlier there had almost been war between the two countries. When the enmity came to a head and the only solution seemed to be war, the frightened Prussian king backed down. In the Treaty of Olmütz (November 2, 1850) Prussia had renounced her ambition to break away from Austrian control. It was the deepest humiliation in Prussia's history since Napoleon had defeated her at the Battle of Jena in 1806. People were amazed when they heard the belligerent Bismarck defend the Treaty of Olmütz. But Bismarck as always was shrewd and farsighted—he knew that Prussia was not yet ready to stand up to Austria. That would come later.

When he came to Frankfurt as Prussian ambassador, Bismarck quickly gave notice of what he intended to do. Every German school child knows the story of the "Battle of the Smoke." According to diplomatic protocol (the set of standards for behavior of diplomats), no guest ever smoked in the presence of a superior officer unless invited to do so. As was the custom, Bismarck came to the office of Count Thun, the Austrian president of the Confederation, to present his credentials of appointment. Count Thun pulled out a big cigar and, without offering one to his guest, began to smoke. Bismarck, always ready for any emergency, promptly took one of his own cigars, which was twice as big, lit it, and blew smoke in the direction of his opponent. This was his way of showing Prussia's defiance of Austria. Whether this story was true or not, it had a point. Fifteen years later, Austria was beaten by Prussia on the battlefield and driven out of Germany forever.

I Life was pleasant and comfortable in Frankfurt. Bismarck remained there for seven years. Here he learned the essentials of diplomacy and served his apprenticeship. He carefully studied his colleagues, both German and foreign. "I find these diplomats," he wrote to his wife, "with their airs of confidence and their petty fussiness, absurd. . . . I am making great progress in the art of saying nothing in many words." He had little use even for Prussian diplomats, one of whom he called "a mousetrap dealer" and another "an empty-headed ass." As for the Austrians, they were "double-tongued liars."*I*

For some years the Prussian king, Frederick William IV, had been acting peculiarly. In the fall of 1857 it became obvious that he was insane. The next year he had to surrender his throne to his brother William, Prince of Prussia, who became regent on October 7, 1858. A new cabinet, consisting mostly of moderate liberals, was appointed. The Prussian people began to speak of a "new era," which was greeted with delight by all parties except the Conservatives. Now, perhaps, the people at long last might get the reforms they wanted.

One of the changes resulting from this was Bismarck's recall from Frankfurt. Hoping to improve its relations with Austria, the new government decided to get the difficult Bismarck out of the way by appointing him ambassador to Russia in April, 1859. He furiously resented being sent "out into the cold" because in his view it was a setback to his prestige. In Russia he learned to know Czar Alexander II and his chancellor, Prince Gorchakov, both of whom sympathized with Bismarck's enmity toward Austria.

By this time Bismarck's constant anxiety and his careless work habits began to affect his health. In the early summer of 1860, he became ill with a serious gastric and rheumatic condition, complicated by an injury he had sustained to his shinbone while hunting in Sweden some months earlier. The leg continued to trouble him in St. Petersburg. In that city he had the misfortune to fall into the hands of a quack doctor, a certain Dr. Walz. The bogus doctor placed a hot stone in the hollow of Bismarck's knee, a mistreatment which tore a vein and opened a large wound. A Russian surgeon then told Bismarck that his leg had to be removed. Bismarck refused, and returned to Prussia wretchedly ill. His condition became dangerous when he suffered a thrombosis and inflammation of the lungs. Tortured by pain, he thought he was about to die. He recovered, but never regained the robust health and strength of his youth. "Since my illness," he said, "I am so exhausted that I have lost all my energy for excitement. I feel like a broken-down acrobat." He became irritable, nervous, and restless, qualities which never left him for the remainder of his life.

Bismarck resumed his duties in St. Petersburg. He expected to be recalled for appointment as minister-president, but instead he was sent by the king to Paris in May, 1862, to serve as ambassador to France. He kept this post for only a few months. Most of his time he spent away from the French capital.

In France, Bismarck had the opportunity of again meeting Napoleon III, Emperor of the French. Earlier, in 1857, when he had been an unimportant diplomatic beginner, Bismarck had had an interview with the emperor and the two had spoken openly of their dislike for Austria. Napoleon III was warm and friendly. He made an offer of an out-and-out Franco-Prussian alliance, but Bismarck could promise nothing. After all, he was still only an ambassador.

The Parisian summer of 1862 was hot and boring for

33

Bismarck. Parisian society and governmental officials had fled to summer resorts. Bismarck was nervous and depressed because the king could not make up his mind whether or not to call him to Berlin as the head of the government. Bismarck now decided to go to London for a few days. He had been there once when he was a young man. Perhaps it might be a good idea to meet important people in the British capital.

In London, Bismarck met the famous Disraeli, and during the course of their conversation Bismarck said openly: "I shall soon be compelled to undertake the leadership of the Prussian government. My first care will be, with or without the help of Parliament, to reorganize the army." Disraeli was impressed, and later said: "Take heed of that man. He means what he says!"

Meanwhile, a critical debate began in the Prussian Chamber on the budget and army reform. After five days, by a majority of 273 to 62, the Chamber refused the money required by the army. King William I, who loved his army, was upset. He would have to abandon old and honorable regiments. He declared to his ministers that it would be impossible for him to carry on any longer and that he was ready to abdicate.

In this situation, General Albrecht von Roon, minister of war, presented a solution. Why not make his friend Otto von Bismarck minister-president? Bismarck, said von Roon, would know how to deal with the recalcitrant Chamber. He was the only man who was willing and able to defy that body, and he did not care whether the constitution was broken or not in the process.

On September 22, 1862, Bismarck arrived at the royal residence in Potsdam for a historic audience with the king. He found the crestfallen monarch seated at a table with his act of abdication, already signed, in front of him. The king asked Bismarck if he were willing to take over the government, even if against the majority in the Chamber and without a budget. Bismarck replied that he was ready.

William I, impressed with Bismarck's bold manner and sensing his complete loyalty, tore up the act of abdication. Two days later, Bismarck became minister-president of Prussia.

Twenty-four years earlier, in September, 1838, the twenty-three-year-old Bismarck had said: "I will play music as I like it, or none at all." From now on his music would be heard—not only by Prussia and Germany, but also by Europe and all the world.

CHAPTER SIX

Minister-President of Prussia: Man of "Blood and Iron"

"I am no democrat, and could never be one."

Otto von Bismarck began his term of office under unfavorable circumstances. He had been called by the king only as a last resort. He had pledged to support the monarch in a conflict with the whole nation. As a result, he was unpopular everywhere. In the theaters and music halls and cafés, jokes about the new minister-president were received with either storms of applause or knowing winks. In foreign countries Bismarck was regarded as a dangerous Junker who was reckless enough to use force on the home front and the sword in foreign policy.

For his cabinet Bismarck picked only reactionary officials who had few qualifications other than loyalty to the king, conservative opinions, and noble birth. The minister-president had no illusions about them—one he called "a liar" and another "a jackass." But he would use them in his own way.

Almost at once Bismarck got into a quarrel with Parliament. He was not worried about the Upper House, the feudal Chamber of Seigneurs, which was conservatively Junker and on his side. But the Lower House, the Chamber of Deputies, which contained the liberal and radical opposition, was different. Here he became embroiled in political battle. The main issue concerned the budget for the coming year, 1863. A committee of the Lower House, consisting of some thirty members, informed the minister-president in plain words that spending money without approval of the Lower House was unconstitutional.

Bismarck appeared before the committee to present his arguments. He spoke with wit and incisiveness. And then came a dramatic scene: he took from his pocket an olive branch and said that he had intended to offer it to the House as a symbol of peace, but he had most reluctantly come to the conclusion that it was a bit too early to do that. He spoke about Prussia's present situation and future task. Prussia, he said, must concentrate its power and hold itself ready for the favorable moment which, too many times, had already passed by. Then came a striking sentence:

Not by parliamentary majorities are the great questions of the day settled—that was the great blunder of 1848 and 1849—but by iron and blood.

Those few words created a sensation. They sped through the German states and around the world. For some unknown reason the order of the last three words was reversed and became "blood and iron" in the popular mind. The impression spread rapidly: Bismarck's real opinion was that the weapons of war must shed human blood before great decisions were possible. The idea of the primacy of "blood and iron" was to give direction to the history of Prussia-Germany for the rest of the nineteenth and twentieth centuries. It was another way of saying "Might is Right!"

Later, Bismarck himself angrily said that his words of 1862 had been misinterpreted. In a speech he made on January 28, 1886, he said what he really meant: "Put the strongest military power, in other words, as much blood and iron as you can, into the hands of the King of Prussia. Then he will be able to carry on the policy you wish. It cannot be done with speeches and celebrations and songs. It can only be done by blood and iron."

Despite this explanation, Bismarck never did live down the words that were associated with his name. People simply believed he meant that blood must be shed and iron used.

The king was disheartened. Only a few days after

Bismarck's speech, the king met his minister-president on a train at a small country station. "What in the world will come of it all?" asked the king. "I can already see my place before the castle on which your head will fall, and then mine will fall, too."

"Well," replied Bismarck, "as far as I am concerned, I cannot think of a finer death than one on the field of battle or scaffold. I would fall like Lord Strafford. And your Majesty would fall, not as Louis XVI, but as Charles I. That is a quite respectable historical figure!"

The king did not find this amusing at all.

Bismarck won his battle with the Lower House by the simple expedient of ruling without a budget. The government continued to collect taxes and duties and spent the collected money for the army. This was unconstitutional, but Bismarck had his way. Fortunately, people were prosperous at the time, and taxes were forthcoming.

The quarrel over money continued year after year. Each year the Lower House rejected the budget, and told the minister-president that he would be responsible for his unconstitutional actions. Each year Bismarck's contempt for the Lower House increased. He still had little use for democracy and constitutions.

There was an ironic and surprising conclusion to this political battle. In 1866, after Prussia had defeated Austria on the battlefield, the Lower House met and voted a "bill of indemnity." In an outburst of patriotism and gratitude for Bismarck's leadership in wars against Denmark (1864) and Austria (1866), the Lower House *legalized his unconstitutional parliamentary rule for the previous four years.*

There it was: recognition that—although he had acted unconstitutionally—Bismarck had worked for the best interests of Prussia. It was a rare abdication of political power by a parliament. Bismarck, whose mood expressed "I told you so!" merely smiled.

CHAPTER SEVEN

War with Denmark, 1864

*"Your Majesty, every one of your immediate
predecessors, even including your brother,
has won an increment of territory for the
State."*

The issue of the duchies of Schleswig-Holstein led to
Bismarck's first war. It was a complicated problem.
Lord Palmerston, the British statesman, described it
this way: "Only three men have ever understood it.
One was Prince Albert, who is dead. The second was
a German professor, who became mad. I am the third,
and I have forgotten all about it."

Let us try to make some sense out of this most con-
fusing situation. As always in history, geography is important.

1. The Treaty of Vienna in 1815 remade the map of
Europe after the fall of Napoleon. Denmark, which was
much larger than it is today, extended down to the
outskirts of the German city of Hamburg.

41

2. The kingdom of Denmark proper consisted of islands in the North Sea and the northern part of the Jutland peninsula. The population in 1864, as at present, was Danish.

3. On the neck of the Danish peninsula, between the North Sea and the Baltic Sea, were the two duchies of Schleswig and Holstein, both about the same size.

4. The duchy of Holstein, the southern part of Jutland, ran from the Elbe River to the Eider River. The important port of Kiel was on the east coast of the peninsula. Because it was close to Prussia, Holstein's people were mostly German-speaking.

5. The duchy of Schleswig lay between Denmark proper and Holstein. It extended down to the Elbe River. The people in north Schleswig were mostly Danish, those in the south were mainly German.

All of these three distinct parts—Denmark, Schleswig, and Holstein—were ruled by the king of Denmark. They were united in what was called a "personal union." Holstein, the southern duchy, was also part of the German Confederation (*Bund*), the union of German states set up in 1815 at Vienna, and including Austria. Schleswig, however, was not in the *Bund* and was not subject to its authority.

Despite these differences, the two duchies, on the strength of a royal decree dating from the fifteenth century, considered themselves to be "for all times united" (*up ewig ungedeelt*). But there were endless quarrels in the duchies between Germans and Danes. In May, 1852, the Great Powers (Great Britain, Austria, and Prussia), tired of having their trade disturbed by the unrest in the duchies, enforced a compromise called the Treaty and Protocol of London. This confirmed Danish control of the duchies, but compelled Denmark to respect German rights. Nobody was satisfied by this solution. There was no peace as Danes and Germans battled one another.

Then came a most serious event—the death of King Frederick VII of Denmark on November 15, 1863. This brought the whole Schleswig-Holstein matter to an acute stage, because Frederick had no children. Who would become his successor in the kingdom of Denmark and in the duchies? The Germans in the duchies hoped that they would now be separated from Denmark.

The situation became more and more confused. On the death of the king, Christian of the House of Glucksburg ascended the throne as Christian IX of Denmark and Duke of Schleswig and Holstein. He did this in accordance with the Treaty of London and by a law which was valid in Denmark and Schleswig, but not in Holstein.

Then a new claimant appeared to dispute the title to the duchies. The day after the death of the king, Frederick, eldest son of the Duke of Augustenburg and the lawful heir of Holstein, announced his succession as Frederick VIII of Holstein. The German people received this news with joy. They wanted Frederick VIII of Holstein to become head of both duchies. But the important question is: What did Bismarck think about all this?

At first he wanted to avoid the issue altogether. Then he got an idea. He would not allow the duchies to be given to either of the two pretenders. *He would take them for Prussia.* This would extend Prussia's seacoast and bring her much closer to the oceans of the world. It was a bold plan by the man of "blood and iron"—if it worked.

Bismarck set to work with great energy and cunning. He was faced with a stone wall of barriers, but one by one he met each problem and solved it. The story of how he did it brings to light Bismarck's genius as a diplomat.

THE BARRIER	HOW BISMARCK REMOVED IT
1. *Denmark*	It could not be expected that Denmark would agree to Bismarck's designs on the two duchies. But she was a small country, and Bismarck decided to rely on force to defeat her. He had to goad the Danes into fighting, for without

44

THE BARRIER	HOW BISMARCK REMOVED IT
	fighting there would be no conquest.
2. *The German Confederation* (Bund)	The German states and Austria were combined in a confederation called the *Bund*. Under Austrian control, the *Bund* would surely protest against Bismarck's scheme to take over the duchies. But the *Bund* was weak. True, it did send troops to Schleswig-Holstein during the critical days, but Bismarck just disregarded them.
3. *The German People*	Bismarck was a little worried about the reaction of the German people, but, by appealing to their sense of nationalism, he soon had them on his side. They became wildly excited by the prospect of a successful war.

THE BARRIER	HOW BISMARCK REMOVED IT
4. *Great Britain*	Great Britain looked upon the integrity of Denmark as vital for the European balance of power. And she was willing to fight for this principle. But Palmerston, the British prime minister, was eighty years of age, and was no match for the aggressive Bismarck.
5. *France*	If Great Britain and France worked together, Bismarck would have been frustrated. But Bismarck cleverly separated the two. Some historians say that he hinted to Napoleon III that, in exchange for France's neutrality, Prussia might give France the left bank of the Rhine. Unable to ignore this bait, the French emperor fell into the trap.

46

THE BARRIER	HOW BISMARCK REMOVED IT
6. *Austria*	Here was the greatest obstacle of all. Austria was the great enemy of Prussian expansion. Bismarck knew that Austria would never permit him to take the duchies. He solved his problem by a simple device—he brought Austria in with him to attack the duchies. It was a master stroke—and it worked.

None of these barriers prevented Bismarck from going forward step by step. He assured anyone who would listen that all he wanted to do was to follow the Treaty of London and keep Denmark free and independent.

On February 1, 1864, Prussian and Austrian troops, shouting "Forward with God!" moved against tiny Denmark. Without firing a shot, they pushed aside the Saxon and Hanoverian troops sent into Holstein by the *Bund.*

The Danes fought heroically for two months. But their small army did not have the slightest chance against Prussian artillery and the new needle guns. On

April 18, 1864, Prussian troops stormed the last Danish stronghold. The little country capitulated.

Bismarck now had no further use for Frederick, the prince of Augustenburg. He dropped him. Bismarck said later: "I hitched the prince to the plow as an ox, to get it moving. Once the plow was in motion, I unhitched the ox."

The peace treaty was signed at Vienna on October 30, 1864. Denmark renounced all her rights to the two duchies in favor of Prussia and Austria. Schleswig and Holstein were placed as a common possession ("condominium") under the combined rule of Prussia and Austria.

Bismarck was delighted. He had won. The Austrians had helped him realize his goal—he would know how to pick a quarrel with them later.

It was all a master stroke—Bismarck had succeeded in taking the duchies permanently from Denmark, without allowing any other Great Powers to intervene. He had made the Austrians accomplices to his aggression, and he had convinced his own king that Prussia was getting only that to which she was entitled. He had also pleased the French emperor. But most of all, and what gave him the greatest satisfaction, his achievement satisfied the German people. There was jubilation throughout the German states. Bismarck had become a popular hero.

All Europe marveled at Bismarck's coup. Such statesmen as Rechberg in Austria, and Palmerston and Gladstone in England, began to see that they were dealing with a diplomatic genius. This man was absolutely fearless and reckless. Lord Robert Cecil, who later became prime minister of Great Britain, described Bismarck's designs on Denmark as "one of the most wanton and unblushing spoliations which history records." How could Great Britain allow it? "England's pledges and threats," he said sadly, "are gone with last year's snows."

Bismarck smiled with satisfaction. He boasted openly about his success. "We do not desire a European war," he said, "but if it comes, we shall not be among the losers. The prospect does not frighten us."

Bismarck was already thinking ahead. He had never forgotten how the Austrians had humiliated Prussia back in 1850 at Olmütz. Here was the next enemy. He would have it out with the Austrians. He would make Prussia the most powerful state in all the Germanies.

CHAPTER EIGHT

The Quarrel with Austria, 1864–1865

"You do not trust Austria. Neither do I."

All during the Danish war Bismarck kept his eyes on Austria—his partner-in-aggression. He never wavered in his intention to remove Austria as the major barrier to German unification. He knew that as long as Austria played any role in German affairs, she doomed Prussia to second-rate status. Only a war, he was sure, could change that. The story of how Bismarck got his war—the second stage in German unification—reveals a political genius at work.

It was a policy of unending pressure—pinpricks one day, massive protest the next, then charges and threats. Bismarck never let the Austrians alone and he made their very existence miserable. Here was the gambler playing for high stakes. If he won, all Germany was the prize; if he lost, he and Prussia would sink into obscurity.

In the summer of 1865 Bismarck intensified his campaign. He demanded that the Austrians agree to the expulsion of the prince of Augustenburg from Schleswig-Holstein. He threatened that, if Vienna did not agree, he would arrest the prince and throw him into a fortress. He sent many messages stating his grievances. He would act alone if he did not get Austria's approval. Meanwhile, he told his generals to be ready. War with Austria, he warned, was only a question of time. Bismarck proceeded toward his goal by four steps.

STEP NO. 1: THE CONVENTION OF GASTEIN. It was typical of Bismarck that, while in the process of pushing for war, he left the way open for his own retreat by agreeing to certain peace moves. He invited Austrian representatives to Bad Gastein, the summer resort where King William I and Bismarck were taking the waters for their health. Here the Austrians, who thought they were getting a peaceful settlement, fell into another Bismarck trap.

The Convention of Gastein, signed on August 14, 1865, ended the joint administration of Schleswig-Holstein by dividing them. Austria was to administer Holstein, Prussia was to rule Schleswig. In this way, Austria got control over land enclosed on two sides by Prussian-ruled areas. Bismarck planned it that way.

51

That was not all. The Austrians agreed that the fortification of Kiel was to be entrusted to Prussia—another victory for Bismarck. What was more, the small duchy of Lauenburg was handed over to the Prussian king for two million thalers in cash—to be paid to the emperor of Austria. This was the first new land which Bismarck was able to offer his king. That grateful monarch conferred a new title on his minister, who became Count von Bismarck-Schönhausen.

The German people were not at all pleased by the Convention of Gastein. They saw it as a crude violation of a principle which both Prussia and Austria had accepted from the beginning—that the duchies be "one and indivisible, forever and forever" (*up ewig ungedeelt*). There was also indignation in the Foreign Offices of both England and France at this display of force. In London, Lord Clarendon called it "the most infamous act since the partition of Poland."

Bismarck was unmoved. Few people realized at the time how shrewdly the diplomatic chess player was thinking ahead. At Gastein he graciously allowed the Austrians to make a vital mistake: they agreed that the partition of the duchies should be only *provisional*. This gave Bismarck the opportunity to open the question at any time he felt like it.

STEP NO. 2: MAKING NAPOLEON III NEUTRAL. Now the cunning Prussian began to wave his net again. His next problem was to get Emperor Napoleon III out of the way. During the week of October 4–11, 1865, Bismarck appeared in Biarritz, a French spa, where the emperor and his empress, Eugénie, were passing the season. Napoleon was suffering from severe abdominal pain which had ruined his physique and which eventually was to bring about his death. A sick Napoleon was no match for the shrewd Prussian.

We do not know exactly what took place between the two men at Biarritz, but we have a fairly good idea. Some historians believe that Napoleon made it clear that he planned to remain neutral and that as a reward he would like to see Venetia given to Italy. Other historians say that Bismarck dangled bait before Napoleon's eyes. He had already offered Napoleon the right to expand his territory "everywhere where French is spoken." Now, he hinted, if Napoleon remained neutral in an Austro-Prussian war, Prussia would look with favor on French expansion into territory on the left bank of the Rhine which belonged to the South German states. Thus, Bismarck was most generous with any land belonging to others. And nothing was promised in writing. While historians are not certain, that is probably what happened. The important thing, however, was that Napoleon III did in fact remain neutral, which is exactly what Bismarck wanted.

STEP NO. 3: THE CROWN COUNCIL OF FEBRUARY 28, 1866. Bismarck's next task was to get the support of his own reluctant monarch. On February 28, 1866, King

William, at Bismarck's suggestion, called a high-level council of his chief ministers to decide Prussia's future policy. Was it to be peace or war?

Bismarck was clear as to what he wanted. He asked for authority to conclude an alliance with Italy and to obtain an understanding with Napoleon III in case of war. Count Helmuth von Moltke, the grizzled old war-horse, was all for war. Only the Crown Prince Frederick opposed Bismarck on the ground that he (Frederick) did not want a "fraternal war" (*Brüderkrieg*). Bismarck argued shrewdly, however. All that had happened in the past few weeks, he said, could be blamed on the Austrians. As a matter of fact, Bismarck was the one who was interfering in Austrian affairs, but he made it appear that Prussia was being repeatedly insulted by the Austrians. He soon got King William I on his side, which was just what he wanted and needed.

Still, King William had his doubts. He ordered the crown prince to write to Queen Victoria of England, Frederick's mother-in-law, and ask her to intercede as mediator. When he heard about this letter, Bismarck went into an almost uncontrollable rage. He did not want the crown prince or anyone else to interfere in high-level politics, which was his own job. He ordered the Prussian ambassador in London to treat the crown prince's letter as unimportant and to inform the British Foreign Office that the duchies of Schleswig-Holstein were indispensable for Prussia. The British decided not to say or do anything. That was precisely what Bismarck wanted.

STEP NO. 4: ALLIANCE WITH ITALY, APRIL 8, 1866. While Bismarck had little use for the Italians, he did not allow this to affect his political sense. For months he had tried to set up some kind of relationship with Italy. He wanted an alliance which would oblige Italy to follow Prussia into a war with Austria, but which at the same time would not obligate Prussia to wage that war. In effect, it was a case of "heads I win, tails you lose."

For the Italians, everything revolved around Venetia, which was then under Austrian control. They would not rest until they got that province, which they regarded as traditionally Italian. Napoleon III was sympathetic to Italian aims—he promised that he would help "to free Italy to the Adriatic." And it seemed to both the French and the Italians that an Austro-Prussian war would give the Italians the best opportunity to obtain Venetia.

The Italians signed a treaty of alliance with Prussia on April 8, 1866. They agreed to join in the war against Austria. But they cautiously put in a clause saying that the treaty would automatically come to an end if Prussia did not declare war *within three months.*

In making this agreement, Bismarck exploded the German Confederation (*Bund*). Its constitution forbade any member to ally itself with a foreign power against any other member. It had been fifty-one years since the *Bund* had been formed, and all during that time no member had ever broken that agreement.

As for Bismarck, he was delighted with his success. He spoke plainly to the French ambassador: "I have convinced the king of Prussia to break relations with Austria. I have concluded an alliance with revolutionary Italy. I have made arrangements with Imperial France. I have proposed in Frankfurt a reform of the Confederation and a popular parliament. This is a success of which I am proud."

Under the constant excitement of these weeks, Bismarck's health began to break down. He was in acute pain from severe neuralgia of the face. Except for the war lords, there was scarcely a German who wanted a war with Austria. The Germans of those days were essentially a peace-loving people who did not like the idea of their sons dying on a battlefield in a war against their Austrian brothers. They sent petitions to the king praying for peace. The king did his best to hold off war. Bismarck assured the monarch that he, too, wanted peace: "It is opposed to my feelings, I may say to my faith, to attempt to use influence or pressure on your fraternal feelings with regard to the decision on peace or war. This is a sphere in which, trusting to God alone, I leave it to your Majesty's heart to steer for the good of the Fatherland. My part is prayer, rather than coun-

sel." Bismarck then laid before his king the "insuper-
able" arguments in favor of war.

Thus, Bismarck talked both peace and war. That was
characteristic of him: he was always careful to leave
two entirely different paths open. He would keep his
eyes on both roads and postpone his decision until he
knew which way would give him the best chance of
achieving his goal speedily and efficiently.

After wars end, they are discussed endlessly in the
history books. Ever since the Austro-Prussian War of
1866, historians have argued about Bismarck's role in
its origins. Did he plan it from the very beginning?
Or was the war, as most German historians say, forced
on Bismarck by Austrian misbehavior? Here is the
judgment of one German historian, Erich Eyck, who
left Hitler's Germany in 1937:

"Bismarck certainly never had any scruples about a
war of this kind, which he himself in later years called
'fraternal.' But it is another question whether he
wanted the war. The answer is that he would have
been willing to do without the war if he had been able
to achieve his aims by normal diplomatic means. . . .

"Thus the conclusion may be reached that, although
Bismarck was not from the beginning bent on war with
Austria, he was engaged in a policy which made war
unavoidable."

CHAPTER NINE

A Would-Be Assassin Strikes

*"Don't be alarmed, my dear, I've been
shot at."*

Was Bismarck forcing a war which the people did not
want? Some thought so. He paid no attention to the
many letters threatening his life. Then, on May 7, 1866,
came a grave incident which showed how deep was the
resentment against him.

Bismarck had been struck by another of his many
illnesses. For days he lay on a sofa with violent pains
in his legs. He complained that he felt "like a wounded
boar." On this May morning he was out for the first
time since the beginning of his illness. He had just
left the royal palace after an interview with the king
and was walking home along the center lane of
the Unter den Linden. Suddenly, when he was opposite the Russian embassy, Bismarck heard two shots
whiz by him. Wheeling around instinctively, he saw a
pale young man behind him coolly raising a six-cham-

bered revolver to fire at him a third time. Bismarck's courage had been tested before, especially in his student duels at Göttingen and when, as a young lieutenant, he had saved his groom from drowning. Once again he acted fearlessly and almost automatically. With one hand he grasped the wrist of the attacker and with the other he seized him by the throat.

Meanwhile, the assailant, struggling desperately to free himself, fired three more bullets, two of which grazed Bismarck's chest and shoulder. Holding his would-be murderer in an iron grip, Bismarck wrenched the revolver away.

People passing by mistook Bismarck for the assailant and nearly attacked *him*. In the confusion, it was natural for them to suspect that the huge man holding the revolver was the aggressor, rather than the slight youth struggling in his grasp. At that moment a company of guards marched by. Bismarck handed his attacker over to them, and they took him off to jail.

As soon as he arrived at his home, Bismarck wrote a short message to the king telling him about the attack. Then he calmly entered the drawing room, where guests were waiting. He whispered to his wife: "Don't be alarmed, my dear, I've been shot at. But no harm has been done. Let us now go in to dinner." Johanna nearly fainted, but managed to maintain her self-control.

The assailant was Ferdinand Cohen, a stepson of

Karl Blind, who had participated in the Revolution of 1848. A fugitive from Baden, Blind was then living in London. His stepson had taken his name. The young student of agriculture, influenced by revolutionary ideas, hoped to save Europe from the threatening catastrophe of war. He would kill the man who was accused of destroying Prussian liberties. During his first night in prison he committed suicide by slashing his veins. The whole story behind the incident never came to light.

Bismarck's family and friends were overjoyed at his narrow escape from death. The king personally offered his congratulations, and a train of leaders of Prussian life followed him. A great crowd gathered in the street to serenade the minister whose life had been spared. The emotional day closed with a speech of thanks which Bismarck delivered from the balcony of his home.

Others, however, sympathized with the assailant and not with Bismarck. A professor at the University of Berlin, the famous physiologist Emil Du Bois-Reymond, while in a bookseller's shop on Unter den Linden, exclaimed indignantly: "How bad revolvers are in this country!"

CHAPTER TEN

The Seven Weeks' War: Austria Versus Prussia, 1866

"Anyone who has seen the eyes of a dying warrior on the battlefield will think twice before he begins a war."

"At this moment our troops are marching into Hanover, Saxony, and the Electorate of Hesse-Cassel. The fight will be bitter. If we are beaten, I shall not return here. I shall fall in the final attack. One can only die once, and if one is conquered, it befits the vanquished to die."

Thus spoke Bismarck to the British ambassador, Lord Loftus, in the old garden of the ministry on June 15, 1866. There was no doubt that he meant what he said. He would not have survived defeat.

The chances of victory were not altogether certain. The Austrian army was strong, and it had German allies. But the Prussian infantry was equipped with the dangerous Krupp gun. This firearm had four times the firing rate of Austrian muzzle-loaders, which required exposure of the firer when reloading. Moreover, the Prussian artillery was equipped with barrels made of steel, not the old-fashioned bronze kind. And Prussian leadership, which included the brilliant General Helmuth von Moltke, was superb.

How would the Prussian troops react when they faced a strong enemy? Could they beat the Austrians and their allies—Bavaria, Saxony, and Hanover? That question was quickly answered. Within a week the Prussians conquered the whole of northwestern Germany and secured their flank. The South Germans, isolated and disunited, were unable to join their Austrian allies.

Bismarck, wearing a steel helmet and a long gray coat, went off to war with the rank of a major of cavalry. He took no part in the management of the army—that was the king's job as commander-in-chief, advised by his minister of war and chief-of-staff. Bismarck, top political leader of Prussia, had no say in military and technical matters. But he was careful to stay close to the king so that he could prevent anyone else from reaching the monarch's ear on political matters.

At midnight on July 2, 1866, word came to the king and his suite that the Austrians were preparing to attack in Bohemia near Königgrätz (Sadowa) with the

Elbe River in their rear. Early the next morning the king, together with General von Moltke and Bismarck, moved to a hill where they could view the battle.

Prussian troops made a vicious assault on the Austrians. But they could not advance against the powerful artillery of the enemy. For the Prussians there was one crucial question—Would the army of Crown Prince Frederick arrive on the scene in time to turn the tide?

On the hill the king and his party could only wait. There was little to be seen other than columns of troops moving in and out of the morning mist. At eleven o'clock came a disappointing sight—the Prussian infantry, having suffered heavy casualties, began to fall back. The alarmed king turned to General von Moltke and asked him what plans he had made for a retreat.

"There will be no retreat," von Moltke snapped. "The fate of Prussia is at stake."

Several hours passed and still the army of the crown prince had not come to the scene of action. Then, at about two o'clock in the afternoon, Bismarck, peering through his telescope, saw toward the northeast what seemed to be a row of trees moving. A great shout went up when it was realized that this was the army of the crown prince. In a forced march he had arrived at the critical moment, and was now rolling up the Austrian flank.

That was the beginning of the end. By 3 P.M. the beaten Austrians were in full retreat. "The campaign is decided," said von Moltke. "Your success is complete. Vienna lies at Your Majesty's feet."

A Prussian officer turned to Bismarck and said: "Your Excellency, now you are a great man. But if the crown prince and his grenadiers had come too late, you would have turned out to be the greatest of all scoundrels." It was a reckless statement that might have ruined the officer's career. But Bismarck said and did nothing about it. After all, the man was absolutely right. Bismarck's position, reputation, and entire life's work depended on the outcome of that battle.

As soon as he was able, Bismarck walked among the wounded. Everywhere he saw bloated bodies, grotesque in the agony of death, and the wounded crying out piteously. Appalled, he turned to an aide and said sadly: "When I think that one day my own son Herbert may be lying that way, I grow sick at heart."

At dusk Bismarck and his party, which had left the king, tried to find a place to sleep. There was no shelter to be found in the inhospitable Bohemian countryside. Walking about aimlessly, Bismarck at one time lost his footing and fell into a manure pit. Finally, he found a spot under a colonnade in the market place of a little village. Here, sheltered from the rain, he slept on a bed made of cushions from a deserted carriage.

Bismarck was delighted by the performance of the Prussian troops. He wrote to his wife: "Our men deserve to be kissed. Every man is brave to the death, quiet, obedient; with empty stomachs, wet clothes, little sleep, the soles of their boots falling off, they are friendly toward everyone. There is no plundering and there is no burning. They pay what they are able to pay, though they have mouldy bread to eat. There must exist a depth of piety in our common soldier or all this could not be."

Two days after the battle, Napoleon III sent a telegram to King William I. It revealed that Austria had asked for France's mediation, that Austria had surrendered Venetia to France, and it requested that the Prussian king conclude an armistice. This was a political matter and it brought Bismarck directly into the picture. He had rather enjoyed the brief respite on the battlefield—it reminded him of the carefree days of his youth—but now there was serious political business at hand.

It was obvious that the French emperor wanted to save Austria by stopping the advance of the Prussian army. It was to his advantage to interfere and to dictate the terms of peace. Would the ambitious Napoleon III send his French troops smashing across the frontier to attack the Prussians in their rear? Bismarck was not sure. But Napoleon failed to move. Nor did he even order mobilization of the French army. This might possibly have been due to his illness—he was so exhausted by pain that he hardly knew what he was doing.

There was still danger because the Russians, too,

might move. The Russians were angered because Bismarck had dissolved the German Confederation, which had been created in 1815, and which had been guaranteed by Russia. Nor were the Russians pleased to see any increase in Prussia's status as a Great Power.

For Bismarck it was a dilemma—How could he avoid intervention by either the French or the Russians? To his acute mind the answer was simple: *He must make peace as quickly as possible.* It was ironic that the man who only a short while ago hotly wanted war with Austria, now became a zealous advocate for peace! The master chess player was at work again.

There was one more formidable barrier in the way. King William I and his generals who had won the war wanted no early peace. They were reluctant to deny themselves the fruits of victory, especially that satisfying triumphant march through the streets of Vienna. The king was a special problem. For a long time Bismarck had drilled into him the idea that Prussia had been forced into an unwanted war. Now William was intoxicated by victory. "I have the thankless task," complained Bismarck, "of pouring water into his wine and bringing home to him the truth that we do not live alone in Europe but with three neighbors." Bismarck told the king that it was important not to annex any Austrian territory and to give the Austrians as easy a peace as possible.

The stubborn king argued violently with his minister. On one occasion Bismarck, in his own words, "leaped up, ran out, slammed the door, lay down on the bed, and howled like a dog." Again and again the emotional Bismarck was shaken by fits of weeping. Perhaps they were false tears. At any rate the king was bewildered and confused, no doubt thinking that if his brilliant minister was moved to tears he must have had real reason for them. William finally gave in and agreed to a cessation of hostilities. He was not too happy about it: "I have been forced to bite into a sour apple before the very gates of Vienna."

The terms of the preliminary peace of Nikolsburg (July 26, 1866) and the final peace of Prague (August 23, 1866) were moderate. Austria was left territorially intact. Bismarck did not want to make a permanent enemy of the Hapsburg monarchy. "We shall need Austria's strength in the future for ourselves," he said. It was a wise decision.

Bismarck had accomplished his task—he had put the Austrians out of Germany. Austria was left to contend with her own nationalities, a struggle which she never solved and which eventually would lead to her downfall. Prussia was now the greatest power in central Europe. And this was the work, almost singlehanded, of the man of "blood and iron."

Now Bismarck soared to a new plane of popularity.

He became the great hero of the German people, the Siegfried who had led them to spectacular triumph. In gratitude, the Prussian *Landtag* voted a donation of 40,000 thalers to Bismarck to be used in purchasing the estate of Varzin in Pomerania. This became a new home for the Bismarcks.

On September 1, 1866, Bismarck appeared before the Prussian *Landtag* and, in a witty mood, asked for a bill of indemnity legalizing his actions in ruling unconstitutionally from 1862 to 1866. He expressed no regrets, but merely asked for a law righting the wrong he had done. The bill was passed by a vote of 230 to 75, a distinct triumph for Bismarck. The irrepressible Bismarck, after the vote was announced, stated that he would repeat the same unconstitutional procedure if similar conditions rose again.

The next year, in 1867, Bismarck consolidated Prussia's position by creating the North German Confederation, a union of twenty-two states and principalities of north and central Germany. The constitution of the Confederation, most of it written by Bismarck himself, was similar to the one adopted by the Second German Reich in 1871. It made the Confederation chancellor—meaning Bismarck—the responsible minister and the political and administrative head of the government. There was a coating of democratic suffrage, but the people were really deprived of actual power. Instead of a parliamentary government, Germany received a veiled absolutism. "Let us put Germany in the saddle," Bismarck said, "and she will know how to ride."

Everything seemed to be going well for the happy Bismarck. But there were long shadows from the west coming all the way from Paris.

CHAPTER ELEVEN

The Road to War with France

"I shall be glad to fight against Bonaparte
until the dogs lick up the blood."

All the world knew that there was growing danger of war between France and Prussia. There was distrust and suspicion on both sides. Emperor Napoleon III felt that French supremacy in Europe had been shaken by the rapid rise of Prussia. French military leaders were not inclined to wait until Prussia should become too strong. The chances were that France would oppose by the sword any attempt to achieve the unity of all Germany.

Bismarck was the key factor on the Prussian side. He believed that the unity of Germany had been only half completed. The southern German states, still isolated, were not anxious to join a united Germany. Bismarck had managed to cut down some tariff barriers between the German states, but that was as far as he could go. Yet what if the French made an unprovoked

70

Otto von Bismarck in 1826 at the age of eleven. From the age of eight to thirteen, young Bismarck was a pupil at Plamann's Institute in Berlin. The high intelligence of the future Chancellor is already revealed in the youthful face. (Painting by F. Kruger; Photographische Gesellschaft, Berlin)

Silhouette of Bismarck as a student at Göttingen in 1832

The student Bismarck at Berlin University in 1834. (Sketch by G. von Kessel; Bong, Berlin)

The twenty-year-old barrister at the Municipal Court in Berlin, 1835. (Watercolor by G. von Kessel)

Prussian ambassador in St. Petersburg, 1859. Bismarck represented Prussia as ambassador to Russia from 1859 to 1862. (Photograph by Elise Wolff)

Bismarck in 1865 after the war with Denmark. (Atlantic-Photo, Berlin)

The Berliner Peacock. "No wonder that he is proud!" Bismarck in Austrian caricature. Berg's Kikeriki, *August 15, 1870.*

The victor of Sédan, 1871. (Photograph by Loescher & Petsch; K. A. Berg, Berlin)

Bismarck in 1877. (Photograph by Loescher & Petsch; K. A. Berg, Berlin)

"Keeping it Down." (Punch, September 28, 1878)

"The Children's Bismarck." Felix Regamey, a French artist, gives an easy lesson on how to draw Bismarck.

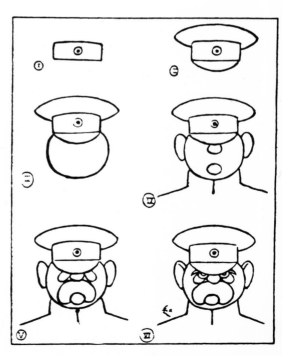

"At evening at Bis-marck's home." (Klad-deradatsch, *1881)*

GOOD WEATHER

CHANGEABLE

STORMY

"Parliamentary barome-ter." This famous Klad-deradatsch *cartoon, published in 1881, ad-vised every minister and Reichstag delegate to watch Bismarck's fa-mous three hairs to as-certain his mood.*

den Russen

den Oesterreichern

den Klerikalen

den Sozialdemokraten.

"Recommendations for the Barbers' Convention." Cartoonists loved to depict Bismarck's famous three hairs. In this drawing, four types of hairstyles are recommended to the Chancellor to attract the sympathy of either Russians, Austrians, clergymen, or Social Democrats.

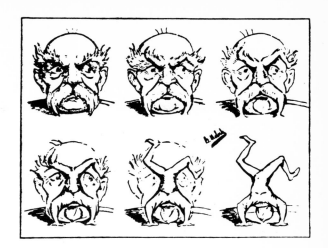

"Bismarck: the man of flip-flops." The face of the German Chancellor as seen by the French cartoonist Moloch, in Révue Encyclopédique, No. 4.

Bismarck and his dogs at Friedrichsruh, 1886. (Photograph by A. Brockmann; Ullstein, Berlin)

"*Dropping the pilot.*" Punch, *March 29, 1890. One of the most famous cartoons of all time shows Bismarck, the pilot, leaving the ship of state. The young Emperor William II, now in responsible command, leans over the side to witness the departure.*

"The retired Chancellor turns in his three hairs, 1890." Throughout Bismarck's career the satirical German magazine Kladderadatsch *had depicted Bismarck again and again with his three hairs. In the issue of March, 1890, Bismarck is shown relinquishing his "insignia" as he departs for Friedrichsruh.*

"The giant returns home." (Figaro, *April, 1890*)

" 'Three Ottomen' at Friedrichsruh." A German cartoon shows three visitors to Friedrichsruh honoring the retired Chancellor, as their legs spell "Otto."

The retired Chancellor at Friedrichsruh, 1890. (Photograph by J. Braatz; Scherl, Berlin)

The titan of Friedrichsruh, 1894. (Photograph by Karl Hahn; Photographische Gesellschaft, Berlin)

attack? If they did, Bismarck was sure that all the German states would unite behind him in a wave of national emotion. All differences that had kept the German states divided for centuries would then vanish.

In his memoirs, *Reflections and Reminiscences*, Bismarck told how, in the spring of 1870, the peaceful Germans, unwillingly and reluctantly, were drawn toward war by French insolence. It was just a political affair, he said. The Germans had to draw their sword to defend their national honor. The French were to blame for standing in the way of German unity.

That was the situation from Bismarck's point of view. There is another way of looking at exactly the same set of facts. Some historians say that Bismarck set a trap for Napoleon III and that the French emperor fell into it. Actually, by the time Bismarck was finished, he had the French *declaring war on Prussia*—a war which *he* thought necessary in order to complete German unification. In making historical judgments, much depends on where the observer is standing.

The issue revolved around what is called the Hohenzollern candidature for the throne of Spain. In 1868 there had been a revolution in Spain which had driven Queen Isabella from the country—and with her, the House of Bourbon. The Cortes, the Spanish National Assembly, led by General Juan Prim, the war minister, began to look around Europe for a suitable monarch to take over the rather shaky throne. Above all, they wanted a Roman Catholic prince of royal background.

Earlier, in 1866, without informing Russia, Austria, or Turkey, Bismarck had sent Prince Charles of Hohenzollern-Sigmaringen to Bucharest to take over the vacant throne of the newly created monarchy of Rumania. Charles was a member of the Sigmaringen stem of the Hohenzollern family. This branch was Roman Catholic, while the royal Hohenzollern line was Protestant. No member of the family, no matter how distant a relative he was, had the right to accept a throne without the permission of the king of Prussia, the head of the royal family.

Bismarck now decided that Prince Leopold, a brother of Prince Charles, would be a most satisfactory king for Spain. Then came an involved series of mysterious negotiations. Inside Spain, State Counselor Eusebio de Salazar began a campaign to bring Prince Leopold to the throne. (Was it possible that German money from a fund controlled by Bismarck was being used to bribe members of the Cortes?) In September of 1869, Salazar journeyed to Germany to offer the Spanish crown to Leopold.

Bismarck, as well as the Prussian ministers and generals, was all for bringing this about. King William I, on the other hand, who knew that there was danger of war with France, was resolutely opposed to the plan. He was sure that Napoleon III would never give his consent and, according to tradition among European royal families, the French emperor had a right to be consulted in this important matter. William told Bismarck that he was against it. Such a royal decision should have ended the scheme, but Bismarck was in no mood to accept defeat. He went ahead as if nothing had happened to bar his way. So, after many delays, Prince Leopold finally agreed to go to Spain. Bismarck then intensified his demands on King William. The latter finally, "with a heavy, very heavy heart," consented.

The procedure to bring off the affair was to be secret. The plan was to have the Spanish Cortes put through the election of a Hohenzollern to the throne of Spain so quickly that all Europe would learn about it only after it was an accomplished fact.

Word leaked out to the French. No one knows exactly how it happened, but apparently a Prussian cipher clerk, who had grown sleepy in the summer heat, got his dates muddled in an official dispatch and released the news prematurely. Whatever the reason, the Agence Havas, a French news chain, had the story and the secret was out.

France was thrown into an uproar. Ever since 1866, French feeling against Prussia had been growing. Now the unbelievable news from Madrid caused the greatest excitement. The French emperor was appalled by what he regarded as an unspeakably low trick. If the Hohenzollern candidature went through, it meant that

73

France would be encircled by Prussian power and might even have to fight a war on two fronts. Napoleon III could not allow that. He would have to do something drastic or his own throne would be in danger. People would compare him to his uncle, the great Napoleon Bonaparte. What would the conqueror have done under such provocation?

At this point, the French foreign minister, the Duke de Gramont, certain that he was supported by the public, made a serious mistake. On July 6, 1870, he made a sensational speech before the Chamber of Deputies: "We will not tolerate a foreign power placing one of its princes on the throne of Charles V and thus disturbing the balance of power. . . . With your support, gentlemen, and that of the nation, we shall know and do our duty without weakness or hesitation." This was supposed to be only a sharp warning to Bismarck, but in both the French and German press it appeared to be a threat. It was dangerous business.

At this time Bismarck was in Varzin, where he had contracted jaundice. He had become so ill that it hurt him "either to speak or hear a single word." He was not excited by Gramont's clumsy speech and he did not attach too much importance to it. He would merely wait until announcement of the election to the Spanish throne came from Madrid, and then things would quiet down. Many years later, Bismarck was to say that Gramont's speech was "an official international threat made with the hand on the sword hilt." Thus, from the perspective of time, he decided that he had resolved on war *after* Gramont's speech.

Meanwhile, King William I, who wanted to avoid conflict with France, worked for withdrawal of the candidature. On July 12, 1870, Leopold did in fact resign. The matter seemed ended.

To Bismarck this was a humiliating blow, a diplomatic defeat. He refused to accept it. He would take the offensive again even if it meant a declaration of war. It was a matter of prestige from which he could not retreat.

Unexpectedly, Bismarck was rescued from his dilemma by Napoleon III, who made a foolish error. Had the French emperor stopped at this point he would have been acclaimed by the whole world for a great diplomatic victory. Instead, he decided to rub salt into the wound. He would extract a promise from the Prussian king *never again to allow Prince Leopold to renew his candidacy for the Spanish throne.*

King William was at Bad Ems on a holiday. While walking in the gardens, he was approached by Vincent Benedetti, the French ambassador, who requested him to abandon once and for all any claim to the throne of Spain. It was a highly irregular procedure. The Prussian monarch telegraphed a calm account of the meeting to Bismarck in Berlin.

When the telegram arrived, Bismarck was dining

with General von Roon and General von Moltke. All three were depressed and had little appetite. Their country had been humiliated. The two generals became even more gloomy when Bismarck read the telegram to them. Bismarck then went into the next room and rewrote the dispatch in shortened form. He did not *change* the words but he left out much and conveyed to the reader an entirely different impression. Then he returned and read his altered version to the two generals. They were delighted: their appetites returned immediately. Bismarck gave the altered telegram to the press (the original text was sent by Heinrich Abeken, German councillor of legation at Paris):

ORIGINAL TEXT OF THE EMS TELEGRAM	BISMARCK'S EDITED VERSION
Ems, July 13, 1870 TO THE FEDERAL CHANCELLOR, COUNT BISMARCK, No. 27, No. 61 EOD. 3:10 P.M. (STATION EMS: RUSH!) His Majesty the King writes to me: "M. Benedetti intercepted me on the Promenade in order to demand of me more insistently that I should authorize him to telegraph immediately to Paris that I shall obligate myself for all future time never again to	After the reports of the renunciation by the hereditary Prince of Hohenzollern had been officially committed by the Royal Government of Spain to the Imperial Government of France, the French Ambassador presented to His Majesty the King at Ems the demand to authorize him to telegraph to Paris that His Majesty the King would obligate himself for all future time never again to give his ap-

ORIGINAL TEXT OF THE
EMS TELEGRAM

BISMARCK'S EDITED VERSION

give my approval to the candidacy of the Hohenzollerns should it be renewed. I refused to agree to this, the last time somewhat severely, informing him that one dare not and cannot assume such obligations *à tout jamais.* Naturally, I informed him that I had received no news as yet, and since he had been informed earlier than I by way of Paris and Madrid he could easily understand that my Government was once again out of the matter."

Since then His Majesty has received a dispatch from the Prince [Charles Anthony]. As His Majesty informed Count Benedetti that he was expecting news from the Prince, His Majesty Himself, in view of the abovementioned demand and in consonance with the advice of Count Eulenburg and myself, decided not to receive the French envoy again but to inform him through an adjutant that

proval to the candidacy of the Hohenzollerns should it be renewed.

His Majesty the King thereupon refused to receive the French envoy again and informed him through an adjutant that His Majesty had nothing further to say to the Ambassador.

77

ORIGINAL TEXT OF THE EMS TELEGRAM	BISMARCK'S EDITED VERSION
His Majesty had now received from the Prince confirmation of the news which Benedetti had already received from Paris, that he had nothing further to say to the Ambassador. His Majesty leaves it to the judgment of Your Excellency whether or not to communicate at once the new demand by Benedetti and its rejection by our ambassadors and to the press. [Signed] A [beken] 13.7.70	

In General von Moltke's words: "Before it sounded like a *Chamade* [a retreat], now it is a *Fanfare!*" In its abbreviated form the dispatch, in truth, gave the impression of an ultimatum. Both the French and German people interpreted it as an insult. *France declared war on Prussia on July 19, 1870.*

Historians have argued to the present day about the Ems dispatch. Some call it an "unscrupulous falsification." Bismarck, they say, deliberately made his selection of words in such a way as to produce on public opinion the exact effect he wished for his own policy. They denounce it as a crude, dishonest, unethical trick.

Other historians defend Bismarck for his editing of

the Ems telegram. They say that it was the only way he could answer French insults. It was not a *falsification*, they say, because he did not change a single word: he merely cut out superfluous words. More than that, they charge, the original statement itself was a call to arms. The French had insulted the aged Prussian king publicly in his own country, and Bismarck had the right to strike back at them in any way he could.

And what can be said about the Hohenzollern candidature? Here again historians differ. One side says that the entire matter developed independently of Bismarck, that he could not in any way presuppose what happened, and that he merely acted to meet each new development as it arose.

The other side is convinced that Bismarck arranged the whole business of the Hohenzollern candidature with the intention of putting Napoleon III in a dilemma: either the French ruler would suffer a political defeat which would eventually cost him his throne, or he would have to go to war. Therefore, argue these critics, the responsibility rests mainly on Bismarck, because he alone kept the initiative by knowing beforehand exactly how Napoleon would react to his moves.

Later, in a moment of depression, Bismarck himself made this gloomy statement: "Without me three great wars would not have happened and 80,000 men would not have perished."

CHAPTER TWELVE

The Franco-Prussian War, 1870–1871

"Napoleon III was cast down by God's mighty hand."

Bismarck presented an astonishing sight as he went off to war. The chancellor of the North German Confederation was dressed in the blue greatcoat of the Heavy *Landwehr* Cavalry. Perched on his head was the familiar steel *Pickelhaube,* that spiked helmet which gave its wearer a decided bellicose look. The upper parts of his legs were covered with long boots, which had been fashionable in the early seventeenth century.

At Mainz, Bismarck joined King William and his entourage. He would not let the king out of his sight for fear that someone else might gain the royal ear. This was Bismarck's war, and he wanted to run it his own way politically. For the next few months the seat of the Prussian government was on French soil.

The flurry of physical activity had a remarkable effect on Bismarck. His health always had been weak. He suffered from blinding neuralgia and many different ailments, but, suddenly, during this campaign, his health improved. The steady routine, the limited amount of food, the long hours in the open air—all these things renewed his physical strength. His main vice was drinking, and here he had no intention of cutting down. After one battle an eyewitness wrote: "After the victory Bismarck began to do some heavy drinking. That is Germania!"

Bismarck was proud of his two sons and, at the same time, was very worried about them. Herbert and Wilhelm served as dragoons in the Cuirassiers of the Guards. Because they were privates, the chancellor could boast that there was no favoritism for his family in the Prussian army.

There was one chilling incident during the evening of August 16, 1870. Bismarck received the news that Herbert had been killed in an attack and his other son, Wilhelm, badly wounded. Quietly, but with a racing heart, he mounted his horse and set out to find them. The following dawn he found Herbert, with a slight wound in his thigh, lying on some straw. Wilhelm was not even hurt. The father was delighted. Only after the war had gone on for some time and they had taken part in many battles did Bismarck's sons receive commissions as officers.

On August 18, Bismarck, at the side of the king, watched the battle at Gravelotte. That bloody day placed nearly every Junker family in mourning. At one point the chancellor himself was nearly captured in the fighting.

The front moved gradually from Gravelotte to Sedan. Here Napoleon III moved among his troops through the drifting smoke clouds. The French emperor, a sick man, should never have been on the battlefield. He could hardly sit on his horse. On one occasion a shell exploded so near him that his face was blackened.

By September 1, 1870, the French had been soundly beaten. The next morning Napoleon III surrendered with 84,000 men. Bismarck himself described the historic scene. He was awakened before daylight by a messenger who told him that the French emperor had left Sedan and was ready to receive him. Bismarck, unshaven and without breakfast, went off at once. Astride his horse, he rode down the path at a high gallop. Ahead of him he recognized the emperor in his carriage. Bismarck rode up, dismounted, and saluted, after which he courteously removed his hat. "Your Majesty commands?" he asked.

Napoleon III, who had come to plead for his army,

asked to see the Prussian king. Perhaps a personal interview between the two monarchs would gain him more favorable surrender terms. Bismarck, who grasped the situation perfectly, wanted no meeting between the two sovereigns until the surrender was signed. It was impossible, he said, for William I was ten miles away.

Napoleon III and Bismarck then went to a workman's cottage by the roadside. There they sat in a ten-foot-square room which contained only a wooden table and two rush-bottomed chairs. Later they sat smoking in front of the cottage. Bismarck described the scene in a letter to his wife:

"A wonderful contrast to our last meeting in the Tuileries. Our conversation was difficult, if I were to avoid matters which would be painful to the man who had been struck down by the mighty hand of God. He first lamented this unhappy war, which he said he had not desired; he had been forced into it by the pressure of public opinion. I answered that with us also no one, least of all the King, had wished for the war. We had looked on the Spanish affair as Spanish and not as German."

Bismarck's account made it sound almost friendly. But then came the jockeying for position. Napoleon III asked for more favorable terms, but Bismarck refused on the ground that it was a military question beyond his powers. When Bismarck inquired if the emperor

83

wished to negotiate for peace, Napoleon replied that he could not discuss that matter as he was a prisoner of war. Bismarck should take it up, he said, with the government in Paris.

Both the Frenchman and the Prussian wanted a quick peace, but it was not to be. A revolution broke out in Paris. Napoleon III was dethroned and a provisional government was established. The new regime announced grandly that it would resist until the invaders were driven from the land. But soon it was engulfed in a wave of troubles.

Bismarck, with the Prussian army at Versailles, decided to lay Paris under siege. After all, he was in no hurry. He would let Frenchmen kill one another in their revolution while he starved the country into surrender. Several times M. Jules Favre, French minister of foreign affairs, visited Bismarck in the hope of obtaining easier surrender terms. A French observer described the two men:

"I was at the outset struck by the contrast between the two negotiators. Count Bismarck wore the uniform of the White Cuirassiers, white tunic, white cap, and yellow band. He looked like a giant. In his tight uniform, with his broad chest and square shoulders and bursting with health and strength, he overwhelmed the stooping, tall, miserable-looking lawyer with his frock coat, wrinkled all over, and his white hair falling over his collar. A look, alas, at the pair was sufficient to distinguish between the conqueror and the conquered, the strong and the weak."

Bismarck became more and more impatient as the war dragged on into the year 1871. In Paris, French government troops and Communards, the Communists of the day, were slaughtering each other in the streets. Bismarck's attitude hardened. He ordered that no more prisoners of war be taken because "corpses need no shelter or food," that French African troops be killed on sight, and that snipers be executed as soon as they were caught. Prussian troops, he said, should fire on starving women and children who came from Paris to Versailles to beg for food and mercy. "I attach no great importance to human life," he said, "because I believe in another world. If we were to live three or four hundred years, that would be another matter."

January 18, 1871, cold and wintry, was one of the most notable days in German history. The streets of Versailles reverberated with the sound of marching boots, the shrill whistles of pipes, and the measured beat of drums. In the vast Hall of Mirrors inside the palace of Versailles, that magnificent structure built for Louis XIV, a platform was set up. Here, surrounded by the battle flags of victory and by representatives of his regiments, stood King William I of Prussia.

After introductory speeches, Bismarck in a low, measured tone proclaimed the new German Empire, unified at last. William I, now king of Prussia *and* German emperor, stepped down from the platform. Avoiding Bismarck, he walked to his generals to receive their congratulations. He did not speak to his chancellor. "It was," he said later, "the most unhappy day of my life."

Why? Why should the Prussian king have been so miserable on this momentous occasion? It was because of an almost ridiculous quarrel over a title. The king wanted to be called "Emperor of Germany." Prussia was everything to him, much more than Germany. He thought of himself first as a Prussian, and then as a German. He held a strong position as king of Prussia, and he feared that as "German Emperor" he would lose power. He had no way of knowing at the time that Bismarck would make the German emperor greater in power and prestige than the Prussian king.

Why did Bismarck oppose the title "Emperor of Germany"? As usual he was thinking ahead. He knew that the other German princes were a jealous lot. He always had had a difficult time getting along with them, but he knew that he had to have their support in the new German Empire. And he was certain that they would object to the title of "Emperor of Germany" because that designation implied a claim on their territories which they were not willing to grant. They would not object, however, to the term "German Emperor."

Bismarck got his way in this quarrel, but only over the furious objections of William I. The latter was enraged for many months over what he regarded as a betrayal by his friend Bismarck. All the same, it was necessary to reward his new imperial chancellor. He raised Bismarck to the rank of prince.

Paris fell. The prolonged siege of the city was over and all French resistance ended. The final peace was signed in Frankfurt-am-Main on May 18, 1871. Bismarck was in no mood to give the French an easy peace, as he had once given the Austrians. He would teach them a lesson they would never forget. The French had to pay an indemnity of 5,000,000,000 francs. They had to give up Alsace-Lorraine, the rich provinces "in-between France and the Germanies" over which the two peoples had been fighting for a thousand years. It was a disastrous and humiliating defeat for the French, and they never forgot it.

All Germany went wild with joy. The historian Heinrich von Sybel wrote: "Tears run down my cheeks. By what have we deserved the grace of God, that we are allowed to see such great and mighty deeds? What for twenty years was the substance of all our wishes and efforts is now fulfilled in such an immeasurably magnificent way."

There were more honors for the great hero of the German people. The emperor gave Bismarck a great estate at Friedrichsruh in the Sachsenwald near Hamburg. This property was ten times the size of the Bismarck family homestead at Varzin. Nothing was too good for the man who had made this victory possible.

Bismarck's work was crowned with success. And it all had been done in only nine years. In that short time he had achieved the unification of Germany—a task that had defied every other statesman in German history. In 1862 he had started work with a depressed monarch who had been ready to abdicate his throne, and now he had made William I the most powerful ruler in Europe. He had taken firm leadership of Prussia, which up to then had only moderate influence in the Germanies and Europe, and he had made that state the unchallenged leader of a united Germany.

Millions of his fellow countrymen now saw Bismarck as the most brilliant German of all time, a genius of everlasting glory. The whole world soon became familiar with the face of the great man.

CHAPTER THIRTEEN

Imperial Chancellor:
The *Kulturkampf*

*"Rest assured that we shall not go to Canossa,
either bodily or spiritually."*

The period of twenty years from the foundation of the
German Empire in January, 1871, to Bismarck's resignation in March, 1890, is often called the Age of Bismarck. During this time he was the generator not only
of German but also of European politics. With a powerful army, efficient governmental officials, and a loyal
middle class, Bismarck was able to prevent any revolutionary outbreaks.

The Second German Empire founded in 1871 (the
first German Empire had been established by Otto I
in A.D. 962) was a federal union of twenty-five states,
each of which, though enjoying a measure of local au-
tonomy, was responsible to the central government at
Berlin. The German emperor, as president of the fed-

eral union, was commander-in-chief of the army and navy and, as king of Prussia, had what amounted to dictatorial control over German affairs. The *Reichstag,* or lower legislative house, was a mere debating society. The *Bundesrat,* the upper house, was composed of fifty-eight personal agents of the twenty-five states. Because the delegates to the *Bundesrat* had to vote as a unit on instructions from their own monarch, and because only fourteen votes were enough to defeat any amendment to the constitution, Prussia, with seventeen votes, dominated that body.

Bismarck was the fountainhead of power in the Prussian government. Appointed by the emperor and responsible only to him, Bismarck selected the administrative officials, directed foreign policy, and played an important role in shaping all legislation. As Prussian prime minister and as German chancellor, he was the single most powerful man in the new Germany.

But all was not easy on the home front. There were bitter rivals and critics. In two major battles on the domestic scene—against Catholics and Socialists—Bismarck lost.

Once Germany was safely unified, Bismarck began to struggle with the Roman Catholic Church. He did not win this time. It is called the *Kulturkampf* (literally "battle for culture," but this is one of those German words that cannot be translated perfectly—it means, roughly, that this was a struggle for control of the minds of Germans).

The difference of opinion between Bismarck and the Catholic Church had begun as early as 1864 when Pope Pius IX, in an encyclical (papal statement) called *Quanta cura,* issued the *Syllabus errorum*—"Catalogue of the Principal Errors of Our Time." This contained a list of modern doctrines which the pope condemned, such as civil marriage and civil education: the Church contended that only marriage inside the Roman Catholic Church was legal, and that education should be in the hands of the Church. There was an even greater stir when the Vatican Council, in June, 1870, adopted the dogma of papal infallibility. This meant that, when speaking *ex cathedra* (that is, "officially as pontiff") on matters of faith and morals, the pope could say or do no wrong. Soon critics of the Catholic Church were charging that the pope claimed infallibility on all, including political, matters.

Bismarck was annoyed and angered by both acts. But because he was busy with his wars of national unification and did not want to quarrel with the Church at an inconvenient time, he decided to await a more propitious moment. Now, with his wars finished, he decided to move. Actually, he was no bigoted anti-Catholic. As an intelligent man he was free from religious hatred. But he looked upon Germany as the birthplace of Protestantism and he wanted no revival of Catholic strength there. His first aim was to subdue all people, Protestants and Catholics alike, to the triumphant power of the State. The struggle, he insisted, was *political*, not religious.

Even more important, Bismarck was concerned about the rising Catholic vote. There had always been a Catholic party in the Prussian Lower House, but it had been comparatively weak. In the new German Empire, Roman Catholics made up more than a third of the population. The new Catholic "Center Party" had become the second strongest political party in Germany. Because it cut across class and state lines, Bismarck regarded it as a dangerous political rival.

While Bismarck did not hate Catholics as a religious group, he was hostile to their political leader. Ludwig Windthorst was a little gnome of a man with a large mouth and a habit of denouncing Bismarck every time he got a chance. He always remained calm while Bismarck lost his temper, and this infuriated the sensitive chancellor. Bismarck believed that Windthorst was disloyal. "Everyone," said Bismarck, "must have someone to love and someone to hate. I have my wife to love and Windthorst to hate."

The conflict soon spread. In the German *Reichstag* a law was passed expelling the Jesuits, those well-known Catholic priest-educators, from Germany. In the Prussian *Landtag* (the state legislature) the May laws were passed in 1873. These laws gave to the State control over both education and the appointment of priests. No one could be a priest in Germany who was not German-born. Another law made civil marriage compulsory. The Catholic clergy was no longer allowed to control inspection of elementary schools.

To Bismarck all this was "a struggle for power, as old as the human race, between king and priest." That conflict, he added, had filled German history during all of the Middle Ages and it had led to the destruction of the old German Empire. "Rest assured," he said, "we shall not go to Canossa, either bodily or spiritually." Most people understood this historical allusion. In 1077, Henry IV, the German king, became involved in a struggle with Pope Gregory VII over the appointments of bishops to office. The astonishing end came when the king, barefoot and clad in sackcloth and ashes, was forced to wait for three days and nights in a courtyard at Canossa in north Italy to beg forgiveness of the pope. With the greatest monarch in Christendom treated in this humiliating way, all Europe understood who was the strongest man of the day. Bismarck proclaimed to the world that no pope would demean him in this way.

It was a ringing boast, but the truth was that, while Bismarck was not humiliated, he really lost his battle with the Church.

CHAPTER FOURTEEN

The Kullmann Assassination Attempt

"This assassin . . . clings to your coattails."

In the midst of the *Kulturkampf* came another attempt on Bismarck's life—an indication of the deep passions aroused by the struggle. In the spring of 1874, Bismarck had suffered another attack of illness, and had been ordered by his doctor to go to Kissingen and drink the health-giving waters there. Every day, at about one o'clock, he would drive in an open carriage from his house to the springs to drink the waters. Invariably a large crowd would gather to see the great man as he rode by.

On July 13, 1874, there was the usual throng lining both sides of the street. Loud cheers greeted the chancellor as he passed. Suddenly a man appeared at the carriage door. Gripping a pistol, he fired directly at Bismarck, who at that moment had just raised his right hand to his hat to answer the cheers of the people. The bullet flew between his hand and his cheek, slightly wounding him in the hand.

Angered, but never for an instant losing control of himself, Bismarck stepped out of the carriage and, amid the loud cheers of the crowd, returned to his house. The attacker, handled roughly by the people who wanted to lynch him, was jailed.

After having his wound dressed, Bismarck insisted on going to the jail to talk to the man who had tried to kill him. His assailant was a journeyman cooper named Kullmann from Neustadt-Magdeburg, who belonged to the Catholic Men's Union, a workingman's club. He had brooded about Bismarck's actions as threatening the very existence of his religion.

His wound was not grave, but Bismarck took seriously this attempt on his life. The next December, in a *Reichstag* debate, he made a monstrous charge against the Catholic Center Party: "You may try to disown the assassin, but nonetheless he clings to your coattails. . . . Moreover," he added, "you will never be able to shake this murderer loose." A Catholic deputy cried out an angry: *"Pfui!"* Shaking with fury, Bismarck replied: *"Pfui* is an expression of disgust and contempt. Don't imagine that this feeling is far from me, too. The only difference is that I am far too courteous to voice it." Later Bismarck said that he was so angered by the term *"Pfui!"* that if by chance he had had a revolver in his pocket, he would have killed the man who said it.

The Kullmann incident did not stop Bismarck, who went ahead with his war on the Church. Bishops were thrown into prison. Priests were deprived of their parishes until nearly half the Catholic parishes had no spiritual leaders. Catholic churches were closed, and neither baptisms nor weddings were celebrated. The large Catholic population complained angrily. The Catholic Center Party began to get more and more votes as the struggle continued.

Bismarck at last realized that this was a battle he could not win. Gradually, he began to retreat by withdrawing most of the anti-Catholic measures he had supported. His reasoning was typically Bismarckian: he would give up his struggle against the "Black International" (the Roman Catholic Church) because he now had a battle with the rising "Red International" (the Socialists). He knew when he was beaten. But he was still bitter about it when he wrote in later years about "light-footed priests pursued through back doors by honest but awkward Prussian gendarmes, with spurs and trailing sabers."

In the spring of 1877, Bismarck, again in ill health, asked the emperor to relieve him of his offices. "Never," replied William I. Instead, the monarch gave his chancellor a long leave of absence. Bismarck retired to Varzin, and remained away from Berlin for ten months.

CHAPTER FIFTEEN

Anatomy of Hate:
The Arnim Affair

*"When I have an enemy in my power I must
destroy him."*

That there was something of the demon in Bismarck
was shown by the celebrated Arnim affair. In hound-
ing a rival and driving him into disgrace, Bismarck
revealed himself at his worst, as a man whose hatred
was not satisfied until he had achieved revenge in full.

Bismarck had known Count Harry von Arnim, a
boisterous giant of a man, from their youth. In 1871
he sent Arnim as German ambassador to Paris, the
most important post in the German diplomatic service.
Soon, differences arose between the two. The clash
hinged around internal difficulties in France, where
there was a struggle for power between monarchists
and republicans. Bismarck, himself a monarchist, had
no use for republics, but in the case of France he pre-

ferred a republic, because he believed that it would weaken that country. Arnim, the German ambassador, much against Bismarck's wishes, supported the monarchist party instead of Adolphe Thiers, leader of the republican forces. When Thiers was overthrown in May, 1873, by the monarchist majority in the French parliament, Bismarck was furious. He turned his resentment against Arnim as a disloyal agent of German foreign policy.

There were other reasons why Bismarck gradually turned against the friend of his youth. Harry von Arnim enjoyed the favor of both the German emperor and the Empress Augusta. Bismarck wildly opposed anyone who tried to stand between him and his emperor. He regarded the Empress Augusta, who liked Arnim, as a personal enemy, and he believed that she favored a monarchist restoration in France. Arnim, he was sure, was working with his enemies—the Augusta clique.

Worst of all, from Bismarck's viewpoint, people everywhere were beginning to speak of Arnim as Bismarck's possible successor as chancellor. This was *the* unforgivable sin: no one, in Bismarck's eyes, had even the pretense of a right to think about himself as the next chancellor. Bismarck would have no rivals for his position.

Arnim denied that he had done anything in Paris to promote the monarchist cause. He complained openly when Bismarck ordered him to change the tone of his dispatches. To Bismarck this was mutiny. He would not tolerate it. He called Arnim back to Berlin in September, 1873, and denounced him. "You're plotting with the empress," he told Arnim bluntly. "You will not stop this intriguing until you are at the very table where I am now sitting. Well, you will see one day that there is nothing to it!"

In February, 1874, Bismarck had Arnim recalled from Paris and transferred to Constantinople. Angered, Arnim began a secret press campaign against his superior. When Bismarck learned about it, he promptly dismissed his unruly ambassador.

Meanwhile, Arnim made a serious blunder. When he left Paris, he kept in his possession a number of documents which belonged to the German embassy there. It was a minor matter, but Bismarck was searching for incriminating evidence. He had Arnim arrested in October, 1874, and brought to trial for withholding important state documents.

It was a sensational trial, publicized all over the world. Arnim was found guilty and sentenced first to three months' and then to nine months' imprisonment. He avoided prison by going into exile. His career was ruined.

In 1875, while in Switzerland, Arnim anonymously published a pamphlet defending himself and trying to show that the attack on him was due to Bismarck's jealousy. Enraged, Bismarck started another action against him—this time accusing him of treason, libel, and insult to the emperor. Arnim was found guilty once again and condemned *in absentia* to five years' imprisonment. The unhappy man, his career blasted, died in a hotel in Nice in 1881 without ever seeing Germany again.

It was really unnecessary for Bismarck to have treated Arnim in this cruel and ruthless way. No one at that time could have moved the chancellor from his solid position. But to Bismarck, any rival was someone to be hated and destroyed. In his memoirs, Bismarck explained that he had not acted from motives of revenge, but only because Arnim had overstepped his authority as an ambassador. As soon as he began writing about Arnim, Bismarck's anger flared up anew. Once again he denounced the man who had long since been dead.

CHAPTER SIXTEEN

The Battle Against the Socialists

"I never include Socialists when I use the word German."

There was little peace in Bismarck's life. There was always some object of his wrath, someone or some party to fight, some political enemy to destroy. As soon as he ended his struggle with the Catholics, he turned his attention to the Socialists. He was concerned about the growth of socialism in Germany. In his earlier years he had enjoyed many animated talks with the brilliant Ferdinand Lassalle, founder of the German Socialist movement. But his attitude changed when the Socialists began to acquire political strength. Now he became convinced that they were a dangerous element dedicated to the revolutionary overthrow of society. He would strike at them first.

On May 11, 1878, occurred an incident that gave

Bismarck his opportunity. As Emperor William I was riding in his carriage through the streets of Berlin, a young workingman named Hödel aimed a revolver and fired a shot at him. The bullet passed harmlessly over the head of the emperor, who was unaware of what had happened. A footman jumped off the carriage and captured the assailant. Hödel was a stupid fellow who had once been a member of the Social Democratic Party and who had later joined Adolf Stoecker's anti-Semitic Christian Socialist Party. There had been no conspiracy by the Socialists. Apparently Hödel, moved by inflammatory speeches, acted on his own.

That was all Bismarck needed. He could count on the support of the public, which had been severely shocked by the attempted assassination of the beloved emperor. Within a week, Bismarck had a bill drawn up forbidding all Socialist agitation and propaganda. The measure was directed only against persons of Socialist conviction, although all Germans were supposed to be equal before the law. The bill quickly passed through the *Reichsrat,* the upper legislative body. But it was thrown out of the *Reichstag,* the lower house, by a large majority. No one voted for it except the Conservatives. Bismarck was furious, but he took his defeat in silence.

Then, only ten days later, there occurred another attempt on William's life. On June 2, 1878, a Dr. Karl Nobiling, a university graduate who had taken a degree in economics, fired a shotgun at the emperor as he was being driven in an open carriage on Unter den Linden in Berlin. This time the emperor, struck by thirty pellets, was seriously wounded. Bleeding from head and arms, and semiconscious, the eighty-one-year-old monarch was taken to the palace. For a while his life was in danger. The would-be assassin, who had no political connections, killed himself before he could be arrested. Again, there was no Socialist plot.

Bismarck was at Friedrichsruh when he learned of the new attack. His first reaction, even before inquiring about the condition of the emperor, was expressed in a triumphant tone: "Now we shall dissolve the *Reichstag*." This was typical of Bismarck, the politician, at work. There was not the slightest ground for supposing that either Hödel or Nobiling had any confederates. There were no plots or conspiracies—these were wild and lunatic actions of disturbed individuals. But to Bismarck this was a chance to make political hay. He would strike back not only at the Socialists but also at the National Liberals, both of whom he regarded as political enemies.

The *Reichstag* was dissolved and a new election took place. Bismarck got the majority he craved. The Conservatives polled some 600,000 votes, while the Social Democrats, who had won 500,000 votes in the previous election, now lost some 60,000 votes.

Bismarck now brought a more carefully prepared

anti-Socialist bill before the *Reichstag*. He called it "the law against dangerous activities of Social Democrats." It forbade all writing or speeches in favor of overthrowing the social order. It called for expelling from the country any Socialist suspected of agitation against the government. There were angry debates in the *Reichstag*. Opponents of the bill succeeded in reducing the period of its validity to two and a half years. Bismarck was disturbed by this amendment because it meant that he would have to apply to the *Reichstag* every second or third year in order to renew the measure. As it turned out, he had to do this four times.

The anti-Socialist laws were strictly enforced. Some 1,500 Socialists accused of political agitation had to serve one-year prison sentences. Many others lost their livelihood. Germany became a vast whispering gallery as informers were encouraged to denounce malefactors to the authorities. Decent people were expelled from their homes in the most brutal way.

Bismarck, unable to distinguish between legitimate political opposition and revolutionary activity, was sure that he was right. He wanted even stricter laws. He went so far as to propose that anyone having Socialist ideas should be deprived of his vote and excluded from the *Reichstag*.

Persecution is a two-edged sword. Here again it achieved exactly the opposite of what it was intended to do. Despite suppression, the Social Democrats gained more and more votes: 550,000 in 1884, 763,000 in 1887, and 1,427,000 in 1890. Bismarck, the master of foreign affairs, had lost another battle on the home front. He was to have no victory over the Catholics or the Socialists.

Later, during the next decade, Bismarck decided to "take the wind out of the sails of the Socialists" by sponsoring social security benefits for the workers—insurance covering health, industrial injury, unemployment, and old age. That system, which Bismarck introduced in the 1880's, is in operation almost everywhere in the world today.

CHAPTER SEVENTEEN

The "Honest Broker":
The Congress of Berlin, 1878

"Every war, including a victorious war, is always a misfortune for the country that wages it."

In the year 1878 Bismarck's public career reached its height. He was the most powerful leader of the proud German Empire. All Europe accepted him as the greatest living statesman. When the Continent threatened to explode into another great war it was Bismarck who stepped in and maintained the peace.

The issue revolved around the centuries-old aim of the Russians to break through at Constantinople to the "warm water" of the Mediterranean Sea. It was a cardinal goal of Russian policy to get to the sea, for they had no warm-water ports to trade with the rest of the world. This desire was frustrated by the British who saw it as a threat to their own Empire. In 1853–1856 the British even went to war in the Crimea to keep the Russians out of the Mediterranean.

The Russians tried again in 1877. This time they struck in the Balkans, the Turkish-controlled peninsula in eastern Europe leading into the Mediterranean. In March, 1878, the victorious Russians forced the Turkish sultan to sign the Treaty of San Stefano, which gave them almost all they wanted. The way to Constantinople was now open. But there the British fleet lay ready. These two Great Powers—Russia and Great Britain—were on the verge of war.

In this dangerous situation Bismarck emerged as a man of peace. He suggested that a great European congress, at which he would preside, be held in the city of Berlin. "We do not wish to go the way of Napoleon," he said. "We do not desire to be the arbitrators or schoolmasters of Europe. We do not wish to force our policy on other States by appealing to the strength of our army. I look on our task as a more useful though a more humble one. It is enough if we can be an honest broker."

"Ehrlicher Makler"—"honest broker"—that was a strange term coming from Bismarck! Gerson von Bleichröder, the chancellor's private banker, told him that there was no such thing as an "honest broker." But whatever the term, the Congress of Berlin marked the turning point of Bismarck's diplomacy.

The Congress of Berlin opened on June 13, 1878, and

ended exactly a month later. A glittering array of diplomats appeared—Benjamin Disraeli (the Earl of Beaconsfield) and Lord Salisbury from Great Britain, Prince Alexander Gorchakov and Count Peter Shouwaloff from Russia, and Count Julius Andrassy from Austria. It was a gathering of sick men. Bismarck, sixty-three, pale and obese, was just recovering from a severe attack of shingles and his nerves were raw. Disraeli, seventy-four, suffering from asthma, bronchitis, and Bright's disease, was confined to his bed several times. Gorchakov, eighty, had to be carried into the meeting halls. Only Andrassy, fifty-three, seemed to be in good health, and he was consumed with hatred for the Russians.

Easily the most sensational figure at the conference was Benjamin Disraeli who cast a kind of spell over the whole Congress. Bismarck was captivated by the charm and wit of the British prime minister. "The old Jew," said Bismarck admiringly, "there is a man!"

That Bismarck found it difficult to control his own tongue was revealed by Disraeli in a letter to Queen Victoria: "In the afternoon at 6 o'clock a great dinner at Prince Bismarck's. There must have been 60 guests. . . . I sat on the right of Prince Bismarck, and never caring much to eat in public, I could listen to his Rabelaisian monologue—endless revelations of things he should not have mentioned. He impressed on me never to trust princes or courtiers, that his illness was not, as people supposed, brought on by the French war, but by the horrible conduct of his sovereign, etc. etc."

Bismarck wanted the proceedings to end as soon as possible so that he could leave Berlin for his summer cure at Kissingen. He would have no delays. He used his power, as president, to force the Congress to finish its work in about twenty sessions.

What to do with Bulgaria brought the Congress to a deadlock on June 20–21. Disraeli, a tough negotiator, wanted no Russian control of Bulgaria, and he seemed ready to go to war on this matter. On one occasion, in the midst of the negotiations, he ordered his secretary to arrange a special train to return him to England. Bismarck, caught between the Russians and the British, was forced to hold private conversations to convince the Russians to give ground. The final decision was to split Bulgaria into two parts, the northern part to become an autonomous state under Turkish control, and the southern area a Turkish province.

It was a triumph for British Prime Minister Disraeli who went back to London claiming that he had brought "peace with honor." (In 1938 another British prime minister, Neville Chamberlain, returned from Germany after the Munich Conference with Hitler, and used the very same words: "Peace with honor!")

The decision to award Bulgaria to Turkish control infuriated the Russians. Now they accused the Congress of being a European conspiracy against Russia under Bismarck's leadership. They denounced him as a "nasty scoundrel."

In his closing speech to the delegates Bismarck said that "within the limits of what was possible, the Congress had done Europe the service of keeping and maintaining the peace." But in private, a few months later, he revealed a more selfish motive when he said that he had tried *"to keep the Eastern ulcer open* and thus jar the harmony of the other Great Powers in order to secure our own peace."

One agreement made at the Congress was to have tragic consequences. Austria-Hungary was given the right to occupy Bosnia and Herzegovina (Serbian provinces) at any time in the future provided that she inform the Great Powers about it beforehand. In 1908, without warning, Austria-Hungary grabbed the provinces. This was a giant step toward the outbreak of World War I in 1914.

CHAPTER EIGHTEEN

The Bismarckian Treaty System

*"What we must do in any foreign policy is
to hinder the formation of any overpowering
coalition against Germany."*

Bismarck's foreign policy was simple—he would consolidate the position he had won for Germany. There had been three wars for national unification and that was enough. He was like a shrewd gambler who, believing that he might lose the next time, chooses to stop playing after a winning streak. Prussia's appetite had been satisfied; now she must digest what she had acquired. Bismarck the great war-maker now become Bismarck the man of peace.

How could Bismarck keep the peace on a continent accustomed to war? He would work to restore the system of European stability that had broken down after the Revolution of 1848. He would set up a system of military alliances. Expecting France to seek revenge, he tried to isolate her from any possible allies. To turn

French eyes from the lost provinces of Alsace-Lorraine he offered France a free hand "within reasonable limits" in North Africa. Meanwhile, he sought to conciliate Great Britain by opposing German colonial expansion and discouraging the construction of a large German navy.

Bismarck arranged his treaties in such a way that it became almost impossible for war to break out. He was the expert diplomatic juggler who kept four balls in the air at the same time without missing one. And it is a fact that, as long as Bismarck's treaty system was at work, there was no major war in Europe. Only after his fall, when his sure hand was no longer at the helm, did Germany slide into dangerous situations which led to war.

How did Bismarck, the architect of peace, construct his treaty system? Here are the steps by which his diplomatic genius worked:

1. *The League of the Three Emperors, 1873.* Bismarck's first step was to bring together three monarchs —Czar Alexander II of Russia (1818–81), Emperor Francis Joseph I of Austria-Hungary (1830–1916), and Emperor William I of Germany (1797–1888)—first in a series of conferences and then into an official league. The sovereigns exchanged promises to act together as good Christian monarchs. If the peace were threatened by any power, the three rulers would consult together on achieving a common policy. In this sense it was a re-

vival of the conservative partnership of the Holy Alliance established in 1815 after the fall of Napoleon.

It was all very vague, but it accomplished what Bismarck, the political realist, wanted. It brought about the isolation of a revenge-minded France. And it implied that the three countries, especially the rivals Russia and Austria-Hungary, would settle their own disputes peacefully.

2. *The Dual Alliance between Germany and Austria-Hungary, 1879.* After the Congress of Berlin (1878), friendship between Germany and Russia broke down as the Russian press began to make bitter attacks on Bismarck. The two countries were on the verge of war in 1879. Under such circumstances Bismarck arranged a secret defensive alliance between Germany and Austria-Hungary. It was agreed that if either one of the two empires were attacked by Russia, the other would come to its defense. Further, if either one were attacked by France, the other would declare its own neutrality.

The formation of the Dual Alliance reveals Bismarck's foresight. In 1866, when the Prussians had defeated the Austrians, Bismarck knew that one day he would have use for an Austrian alliance. That was one of the reasons why, against the will of King William I and the military leaders, he had insisted on an easy peace with the Austrians. In 1879, just thirteen years later, he needed that treaty, and got it.

3. *The Triple Alliance, 1882.* Bismarck completed the framework of his treaty system by extending the scope of the Dual Alliance to include Italy. As bait he offered the Italians a free hand in North Africa, which cost him nothing. He had no illusions about the strength of the Italians, who, he said, had "a great appetite but poor teeth." The secret treaty provided that if any one or two of the partners were attacked by two enemy powers, all three partners would go to war simultaneously.

In setting up the Triple Alliance, Bismarck had several motives: (1) he wanted to prevent France from becoming allied with Italy; (2) he aimed to bring the rival Austrians and Italians together in order to increase his own strength against Russia; and (3) he wanted to give Austria-Hungary a guarantee of Italian neutrality in the event of a war with Russia.

At the same time, the Triple Alliance had advantages for all three partners. For Germany it meant a guarantee against French revenge. For Austria-Hungary it was a bulwark against Russian expansion in the Balkans. For Italy it was an aid to the conquest of Tunis and Tripoli in North Africa, as well as a means of checking French domination in the Mediterranean area.

Thus, the Triple Alliance is an excellent example of the master chess player at work. Bismarck's suspicions of Italy as a partner turned out to be correct. When

World War I began in August, 1914, the Italians refused to honor the Triple Alliance. Their reason was a good one—they were obligated to go to the help of Germany in a *defensive* war, but Germany had *invaded* Belgium.

4. *Reinsurance Treaty with Russia, 1887.* Bismarck's mind was continually at work to strengthen his structure of security alliances. Now that he had a secret Dual Alliance with Austria-Hungary which was directed at Russia, why not conclude a secret treaty with Russia? By "keeping the wires to St. Petersburg open," he would cancel the possibility of war.

This was Bismarckian power politics at its brilliant best. How did he manage it? He called in the Russian representative at Berlin and read to the astonished man the text of the secret Austro-German Dual Alliance. Bismarck again got what he wanted. In the Reinsurance Treaty, signed on June 18, 1887, each party promised the other to remain neutral in the event of war with a third Great Power. The treaty was to be renewed every three years. It was considered to be so secret that neither Germans nor other Europeans heard anything about it until Bismarck himself, in a fit of anger against the next emperor, William II, disclosed it in 1896, six years after his resignation as chancellor. He wanted to embarrass William II, who had failed to renew the Reinsurance Treaty.

Bismarck's treaty system was not perfect. There was

much that was wrong with it and there was always the question of how it would actually work in a serious crisis. But it effectively maintained Germany's strong position on the Continent until the emergence of the rival Triple Entente between France, Great Britain, and Russia (1907). And there was no general European war until 1914, some twenty-four years after Bismarck's resignation.

CHAPTER NINETEEN

Seventieth Birthday

"The longer one lives, the more enemies one makes."

Bismarck's seventieth birthday, on April 1, 1885, was an occasion for celebration, not only by his family but for the German people as well. The great man was enthroned in the hearts of his people. Thousands of telegrams and letters poured in. There were speeches, dinners, and torchlight processions. Communities began to erect tablets and monuments to their hero.

There were songs and odes in Bismarck's honor. The most popular one was:

> *Who built for us the Empire wide,*
> *   Whose bulwarks high uprear?*
> *Germania, Imperial bride,*
> *   Who gave the crowns to wear?*
> *With power, has one*
> *That wonder done,*
> *   Whose might we sing and praise.*

Bismarck at this time was a wealthy man, but still the people wanted to do something tangible to express their admiration. In honor of his birthday, committees were formed throughout the country to collect money for a "present of honor." A fund of more than two million marks (about $500,000) was subscribed. Half of this fund was given outright to Bismarck to be used for any public cause he wished: He directed that this money be used for the benefit of university candidates. The other half was used to buy for the Bismarck family that portion of the original Schönhausen estate that had been lost to it for some fifty years.

All this had an invigorating effect on Bismarck. What pleased him most among the 3,500 telegrams and 2,100 letters from various sources was an autographed letter from his master, Emperor William I. The monarch presented him with a reduced copy of Anton von Werner's painting of the proclamation of the German Empire in the palace of Versailles in 1871. Along with it came this message which Bismarck cherished more than all his other gifts and letters:

Berlin, 1st April, 1885

My dear Prince:

When a strong desire pervades the German people to show you on your 70th birthday that all you have done for the greatness of the Fatherland lives in so many hearts, I feel impelled from my heart to tell you today how much I rejoice that such an impulse of gratitude and veneration for you possesses the entire nation. This gratifies me, for it is an acknowledgment that you have abundantly earned, and it warms my heart to see these feelings manifested to such an extent. It is an ornament to the nation at the present time, and it is a good augury for the future, when she shows her appreciation of the true and great, and when she celebrates and honors her deservedly deserving men.

It is a special joy for me and my house to take part in such a celebration, and we desire to express to you, by the accompanying picture, with what feelings of grateful remembrance we do this. For the picture recalls one of the greatest moments in the history of the House of Hohenzollern, which can never be thought of without at the same time calling to recollection your great services.

You know, my dear Prince, that I shall always have the fullest confidence in you, the sincerest affection, and the warmest thankfulness toward you! I am only saying here what I have often expressed to you, and I feel that this picture will always remind your descendants that your Emperor and King and his house are fully aware of what we owe to you.

In this spirit and with this feeling stretching far beyond the grave, I end these lines, and remain,

Your grateful and truly devoted
Emperor and King

WILLIAM

To this message Bismarck replied in grateful and gracious tone:

Kissingen, June 23, 1885

I thank Your Majesty most humbly for the gracious telegram with which Your Majesty has honored me. The losses which Your Majesty has sustained recently, by the death of faithful servants, are numerous and heavy, and exhort us who are left behind to fill, by increased devotion in the sovereign service and to Your Majesty's person, the empty places of those to whom Your Majesty was attached. It is especially painful to me that my state of health does not permit me to manifest my most respectful sympathy in Your Majesty's affliction by my presence. I am permitted to hope, however, that my "cure" this year will have an especially favorable effect, and already feel traces of increased vigor when taking bodily exercise. This result is due to a great extent by the decreased burden of work. . . .

May God give his blessing to Your Majesty's "cure" at Ems and especially at Gastein this year as in former years.

v. BISMARCK

CHAPTER TWENTY

The Tragedy of Frederick III, 1888

"Heroism, national honor, and above all, hard work in the service of the Fatherland—these characteristics were the legacy of our departed Emperor, William I."

On March 8, 1888, Bismarck brought documents for Emperor William I to sign. The old man (it was just before his ninety-first birthday) had caught a cold and was in bed. He had been weakened by the Nobiling attempt on his life. The two talked for a few minutes and then Bismarck left. "I will see you again," said the emperor—his last words to Bismarck, for he died the next day.

Bismarck immediately appeared before the *Reichstag* to inform the members officially that William had just died. The man of "blood and iron" was gripped by emotion. With tears in his eyes he broke the sad news.

Thus ended the close relationship between Otto von Bismarck, Pomeranian Junker, and his royal master, the Prussian Hohenzollern king whom he had made emperor. For twenty-six years, since 1862, when Bismarck had prevented William from abdicating the throne, the two had worked together. It was a relationship in which the vassal had power of command over his lord. William almost always deferred to Bismarck's judgment. And that judgment was effective enough to propel Prussia and the House of Hohenzollern to power in Germany.

William I was not a great man, but he was a man of honor, loyalty, and courtesy. He did not always understand Bismarck's policies nor did he always approve of them. "At best," he said, "it isn't easy to be an emperor under such a chancellor." At times he would lose his patience and roar like a drill-sergeant at his chief minister.

Bismarck had lost his main supporter. Though he wept, he soon pulled himself together. "And now forward," he said.

Crown Prince Frederick, heir to the throne, was in Italy at the time of his father's death. He returned at once to Germany to mount the throne as Emperor Frederick III.

Frederick was fifty-seven when he came to the throne. People who remembered him as a hearty example of manhood were now shocked by his appearance.

His gray face was shrunken, his once luxuriant beard was sparse. From his neck protruded a little silver tube which allowed him to breathe. His larynx was swollen and his vocal chords were useless. He had to write down whatever he had to say.

What had happened? A year earlier, in May, 1887, Frederick had complained of an annoying sore throat. His doctors suspected cancer, but they did not tell the crown prince just how seriously ill he was. At the suggestion of his wife, the Crown Princess Victoria (a daughter of England's Queen Victoria), a famous English physician, Sir Morell Mackenzie, was called in as consultant. Dr. Mackenzie advised that an operation be postponed. It is not certain whether the English doctor believed that the diagnosis of cancer was incorrect or whether he considered an operation to be cruel and useless at this late stage.

The surgery finally took place, but it was far too late. Frederick was in the terminal stage of cancer when he came to the throne. Only ninety-nine days of life were left to him.

It was a tragedy for Germany. Frederick was a man of liberal instincts who believed in freedom and equality. It is possible that the history of Germany might have been far different had he lived his normal span of life.

Bismarck, always the conservative, had little use for Frederick III's ideas. The chancellor had an even greater dislike for Frederick's English wife (he called her "a wild woman"). Bismarck was convinced that the Empress Victoria was betraying state secrets to her mother, the Queen of England. It was a false charge—the empress could not possibly have had any knowledge of such secrets. She was, however, an observant woman, as testifies this description she gave of Bismarck—one of the most accurate ever made of him: "Bismarck always wants the Germans to feel that they would be attacked, ill used, insulted, betrayed, and sold to their enemies, were he not there to protect them. . . . I love honesty and openness, decency, and simplicity. I am sick of a system that uses base means, even if it be serviceable to so great a man. Certainly he is a patriot and a genius, but brutal and cynical."

The dangerously ill emperor decided to work with Bismarck as well as he could. But within a few weeks Bismarck was deep in a bitter quarrel with the royal pair.

It is called the Battenberg affair. The German Princess Victoria, a flirtatious and impressionable young girl, fell in love with Prince Alexander of Battenberg, a handsome figure in his shining helmet and fine-fitting uniform, and an aspirant to the throne of Bulgaria. Her mother, the Empress Victoria, and her grandmother, Queen Victoria of Great Britain, warmly supported the idea of marriage. They urged the emperor to invite young Prince Alexander to Berlin, give him a post in the German army, and award him a high decoration as steps leading to the marriage.

Bismarck protested in the strongest terms. Battenberg, he said, was only an adventurer. More important, the chancellor was sure that the marriage would disturb the good relations between Germany and Russia. It was a political matter, he said. Bismarck's policy was to maintain good relations with Russia. That could not be done if the proposed marriage went through, because Prince Alexander was detested by the Russian czar. There was another complicating political factor. Bismarck suspected that the great interest which the Empress Victoria showed in the projected marriage was due, not so much to her feelings as a mother, but more to a desire to bring the German Empire to Great Britain's side in the controversy between Great Britain and Russia in the East. Bismarck's view was that the personal happiness of the princess had to be sacrificed in the interests of Germany, and that her marriage to Battenberg should never take place.

The quarrel became serious when Bismarck threatened to resign if the couple married. At this time Queen Victoria of Great Britain came to Germany on a visit, and rather than be accused of interfering in Germany's affairs, she decided to drop her support of the marriage. Once again Bismarck triumphed over the royal family, who never forgave the chancellor for blasting the love affair.

On June 13, 1888, Bismarck saw the dying emperor for the last time. It was a pitiful scene. Frederick could not utter a word, but he stared at his chancellor as he joined the hands of the Empress Victoria and Bismarck. Bismarck understood the message. "Your Majesty," he said, "I shall never forget that Her Majesty is my Queen."

Frederick III died on June 15, 1888. Bismarck, who had a distaste for funerals, did not attend the ceremonies. Soon he forgot all about Frederick's widow.

To the throne came William II, eldest son of Frederick III, and the third Hohenzollern whom Bismarck was to serve. There was trouble in the air.

CHAPTER TWENTY-ONE

The Clash with William II

*"William II is the man who will
certainly ruin the Empire."*

William II was just twenty-nine years old when he became king of Prussia and German emperor. This flamboyant Hohenzollern turned out to be Bismarck's nemesis.

William had had a miserable childhood. Because of an accident at birth he was born with a shortened arm, for which, without reason, he blamed his mother. He never liked his English mother nor her people. His early schooling was directed by a harsh tutor named Professor Hinzpeter. Time and time again the tearful young prince would fall off the saddle of his pony, but would be reseated even though he protested. In this way he was trained to control his body so that, later in life, he could sit motionless for hours on his horse.

As he approached young manhood, Prince William had already developed peculiar characteristics. He had a fine mind but, unfortunately, he had several erratic qualities. Arrogant and excitable, he strutted around in a dashing Hussar's uniform. He was loud, boisterous, domineering, and capable of quick anger, although he could be charming when he wanted to impress others. Sometimes he would burst into uncontrollable fits of laughter. He also had a strange sense of humor: he was delighted by his own practical jokes which other people regarded as either in bad taste or stupid. Above all, he was anxious not to show fear and he would go to any length to avoid being called a coward. For the rest of his life he was given to boasting, excitedly making claims to greatness, or threatening his enemies. Like most bullies, he was a weakling at heart.

Prince William was brought up in a court filled with intrigue and gossip. He was surrounded by ambitious officers of the Prussian guard who flattered him and laughed at his jokes. Interested in diplomacy, he would go to the Foreign Office, ask to see the secret reports, read them, and then make written comments in the margin. In 1886 his father protested to Bismarck: "In view of the immaturity and inexperience of my eldest son, as shown by his tendency to overestimate himself, I cannot but call it dangerous to introduce him this early to foreign questions."

When William II ascended the throne in 1888, he deferred to the wishes of Bismarck for the time being. The young emperor was absorbed in a round of festivities and state visits to St. Petersburg, Rome, and other capitals. He allowed the experienced chancellor to make all governmental decisions, as was done under the preceding sovereigns. But that did not last long. Differences between emperor and chancellor began to sharpen.

Up to this point Bismarck had felt himself secure in his position. Who could challenge his power? Was there anyone in all Germany to match him in experience? He was chancellor, minister-president, foreign minister, and minister of trade. For years he had directed the affairs of state, and every governmental official, no matter how important, looked to him, not to the emperor, for guidance. He, the great Bismarck, had almost singlehandedly united the German Empire and had made its flag respected and feared throughout the world. Could anyone really expect him to submit to the will of this vain and aggressive young Hohenzollern who had just come to the throne?

On his side, William II refused to play a secondary role to Bismarck. Had not Bismarck himself said before the *Reichstag* that the real minister-president of Prussia was His Majesty the King? Any experienced politician knew that this was true only in theory, but William II, tasting power for the first time and finding it sweet, took it as literal truth. He would be the real ruler of Prussia-Germany, and no one, not even the great man, would stand in his way.

The young emperor was supported by the military clique, which praised and applauded him and warned him that he could never become a great emperor as long as he was under Bismarck's thumb. Would Frederick the Great ever have achieved his exalted place in history if in his day he had taken second place to a powerful minister? The world was changing. The old and the new did not think alike. The old man had done a good job—everybody knew that—but he was out of date, past his prime, and resting on the laurels of the old days. Watch the Bismarck family, warned the courtiers. Certainly Bismarck was grooming his adored son Herbert to take his place as the leader of the German government.

All this fell on receptive ears. William II took great pride in embarking on a "new course." He would build a navy which would challenge Britain's might on the seas. (Bismarck was far too intelligent to try that. "We are land rats and the British are sea rats, and the two types of rats don't mix!") William II wanted to build a great German colonial empire (Bismarck was always skeptical about that although he did begin a colonial policy).

There were other differences between the two men. William II fancied himself a friend of labor, and flirted with its political leaders. In May, 1889, when a strike erupted among miners in Westphalia, the emperor took their side and criticized the employers for allowing terrible conditions in the mines. Bismarck, always the conservative Junker, supported the employers. To help the workers by encouraging strikes, he said, was "humanitarian rubbish." There was another way to assist the working class—by the social legislation which he (Bismarck) sponsored.

Emperor and chancellor disagreed on the question of prolonging the laws against the Socialists. Upon the expiration of this bill in 1890, there was a proposed measure to make the laws permanent. Bismarck still distrusted the Socialists. But William II saw no necessity for extending the anti-Socialist campaign. The *Reichstag* rejected the proposed bill. In the bitter general election which followed, Bismarck's political enemies won the victory. The old anti-Socialist laws died.

In foreign policy, too, there was a clash between William II and Bismarck. For years Bismarck had considered it a cornerstone of his foreign policy to maintain good relations with Russia. The Reinsurance Treaty with Russia, signed in 1887, was to expire in three years, at which time it was supposed to be renewed. There were indications that the emperor was unwilling to extend this treaty which Bismarck regarded as vital for the security of Germany.

Bismarck's world was beginning to crack, but he was not aware of it.

CHAPTER TWENTY-TWO

Dropping the Pilot

"Then I am to understand, Your Majesty,
that I am in your way?"

The relations between Emperor William II and Chancellor Bismarck gradually worsened until in March of 1890 the situation came to a head. Above all, Bismarck was determined to remain in office despite his disagreements with the royal will. He did his best to win the other ministers over to his side. On the strength of a previous cabinet order as early as 1852, he forbade any minister to report to the emperor on any matter except in the presence of the minister-president. For many years no one had paid any attention to this decree.

William II, however, saw in the revival of this decree an attempt by Bismarck to eliminate the emperor's usefulness. He demanded that it be revoked. Bismarck refused. There was no compromise—neither the emperor nor the chancellor would give in.

Then the emperor learned (the royal court was always rife with gossip) that Bismarck had been visited by Ludwig Windthorst, the gnomelike, acid-tongued leader of the Catholic Center Party. William, suspecting some kind of political intrigue against himself, went into a rage. What was Bismarck trying to do behind the sovereign's back?

Early on the morning of March 15, 1890, the elderly chancellor, still half-asleep, was awakened and told that the emperor had come and wanted to talk to him. Grumbling, and in a bad mood, the old man dressed hurriedly.

William asked Bismarck about Windthorst's visit. Bismarck immediately admitted that the meeting had taken place.

"I hope you had him thrown out of the door," said the emperor harshly.

"No," answered Bismarck, "it is my duty to receive any member of the *Reichstag* who has made such a request in proper form."

"Even if your sovereign forbids you?"

The chancellor replied that his sovereign's right to say whom he should or should not receive ended at the door of his own wife's living room.

These were insulting words. The interview grew even more stormy. William later said that Bismarck was so furious that he feared his chancellor would throw an inkstand at him.

William then asked if Windthorst's visit had been arranged by the chancellor's Jewish financial adviser, Gerson von Bleichröder, adding that "Jews and Jesuits always hang together." Bismarck replied that Bleichröder was a banker, that he himself regarded Jews as a useful part of human society, and had often used them in the transaction of important diplomatic business. William said that in the future Bismarck should first seek royal permission in such cases when he entered into political discussions with parliamentary leaders.

At this point Bismarck remained silent.

William then demanded abolition of the royal decree of 1852. Bismarck tried to change the subject by talking about the emperor's intention to visit the Czar of Russia. Bismarck advised him not to go because he had reports that the czar's feelings were unfriendly. He had reports about that in his own hands.

Curious, William demanded to see the reports. Bismarck handed him a paper. The emperor's face reddened when he read a document in which the czar had called him (William) *"un garçon mal élevé et de mauvaise foi"* (an ill-bred youngster of bad faith).

That was the end. Bismarck had treated his sovereign like a naughty schoolboy. William again ordered abolition of the royal decree, and stormed angrily off.

Reconciliation was now impossible. The two men, both being of highly nervous temperament, could not work together. Each would tremble violently in the presence of the other. On March 18, 1890, Bismarck sent in his letter of resignation.

The next few days were busy ones for the fallen statesman. Driving to Charlottenburg to visit the tomb of Emperor William I, he entered the solitary vault, and laid a few roses on the tomb of the monarch whom he had served so long and loved so well. Berliners poured out to weep and to wave farewell as the Bismarcks left for Friedrichsruh. A correspondent described it for the London *Times* as follows:

"Cheer after cheer, each louder and more thrilling than the other, went up and made the vaulted station ring as the Prince showed himself at the window of his carriage. In the intervals of the cheering the crowd struck up the *Wacht am Rhein* or *Deutschland, Deutschland über Alles*. At last the excitement reached its culmination when the whistle shrieked the signal for departure, and when, amid a final salvo of frantic cheers, blended with the sound of the Cuirassiers' trumpets, the train slowly steamed out of the station, Prince Bismarck shaking hands from the window all the while. Then the crowd slowly dispersed, and as some of its members neared the Brandenburger Tor they encountered the young Emperor placidly trotting home from his afternoon ride in the Tiergarten."

The whole world was astonished by the news from Berlin. The British humor magazine *Punch* published a cartoon which became famous. Called "Dropping the Pilot," it showed Bismarck, the experienced "pilot," with obvious feelings of anxiety, stepping down the gangplank while leaving the "ship of State." The new "captain," William II, unaware of the perils ahead, leans over the side to watch his departure. The implication was clear—this "ship" would have rough sailing.

And rough sailing it was. Just twenty-eight years later, in the year 1918, the Hohenzollern dynasty came to an end.

CHAPTER TWENTY-THREE

The Wounded Titan in Retirement

"Sunshine and wine are the two most valuable things for an old man."

For Otto von Bismarck it was a devastating tragedy. He was infuriated by the way he had been driven from office. True, he had resigned, but he was always to regard that as a dismissal. For fifty-four years, since 1836, he had served the Prussian state and its Hohenzollern masters. Under his leadership the German nation had become united, strong, and powerful—one of the great powers of the world.

Now he, who had been virtually the ruler of his people, was robbed of everything that made life worth living. He had been cast aside, as it were, like an old shoe. He was now seventy-five years old, but his intellect and energy were as vigorous as ever. At a time when he felt himself fully able to carry on his public work, he was condemned to inaction.

Bismarck retired to Friedrichsruh, the large estate in the Sachsenwald, given to him by Emperor William I after the victory of 1871 against France. Here he lived for the remaining eight years of his life. The large home on the estate was formerly an inn standing next to the railway station on the Berlin-Hamburg line. The noise of the trains rumbling by never seemed to disturb Bismarck. In the early mornings he liked to watch the activities of the birds. Most of all he enjoyed taking long walks alone in the pine woods, for throughout his life he had felt a personal relationship with his trees, and he gave strict orders never to cut down a tree on which birds rested. "If I did not have my trees, I don't know how I could live."

Bismarck preferred the company of dogs to that of humans. He was especially fond of his Great Danes, huge, overbearing animals who quickly made decisions as to whether or not they liked a visitor. Bismarck almost always agreed with their judgment. In the long series of dogs that he owned, his favorite was Black Tyras, whom people called the *Reichshund* (Empire Dog).

It was not, however, an altogether quiet retirement. Friedrichsruh became a kind of Mecca for the German people. Crowds of visitors streamed there, especially on Sundays, in the hope of seeing the great man. They came with presents and plaques, letters and applause. Veterans saluted him, choral societies sang for him, gymnasts performed. Hawkers walked through the village streets selling "Bismarck soap" and "Bismarck snuff," or offering postcards showing Bismarck as a mighty hero hammering out German unity on an anvil. At night there were torchlight processions, and burghers who had too much to drink staggered through the village lanes loudly expressing their love for the fallen chancellor.

Bismarck barely smiled as speakers referred to him as "Otto the Great." On occasion he received large delegations of student groups and societies who came to render homage to him. He spoke to them frankly and courteously.

A spirit of homage gripped the entire country. Bismarck monuments began to appear throughout Germany. Even the smallest village had its *Bismarckstrasse* (Bismarck Street). And "Bismarck herring" became world famous.

All this was fine, but none of it was enough to repay Bismarck for the affront he had received. To the day of his death he never forgave William II for the circumstances of his retirement. The emperor tried to make it appear that the resignation was voluntary and even friendly on Bismarck's part. He conferred the highest honors on the retired chancellor, even raising him to the rank of field-marshal. Bismarck was not pleased by this gesture, but as a soldier he had to obey and accept the honor without question.

It was galling for the old man to see the state which he had fashioned now being run by an arrogant young emperor and his inexperienced crowd of fawning followers. He was angered by changes made in the constitution which he himself had written. He saw endangered his whole system of alliances which he had planned to maintain the peace of Europe. He looked on as his old enemies, whom he had carefully kept away from the center of power, were accepted in court circles. He did not understand this new world nor did he like it.

The angry old man refused to remain silent. He never hid his feelings from newspapermen who came from all over the world to interview him. He told them that he had not been treated with the consideration that he deserved. He criticized his successors for failure to renew the Reinsurance Treaty with Russia, which he regarded as absolutely essential for Germany. He looked with distaste upon a new treaty with England concerning difficulties between the two countries in Africa. "I would never have made that treaty," he said.

Bismarck went far beyond normal political criticism. He made an arrangement with a newspaper, the *Hamburger Nachrichten,* to publish his opinions in unsigned articles. Everyone, including the emperor, knew who was writing these bitterly critical pieces which bordered on disloyalty. The emperor was outraged, but what could he do? Bring the great chancellor to court on formal charges? The criticism was embarrassing, but it was better, perhaps, just to wait until the complaining old man died.

Shortly after his resignation Bismarck began to work on his memoirs. For hours he would dictate to Lothar Bucher, his assistant. The work might have been of great historical value, but, instead, it turned out to be an apology for Bismarck's life and career. The author presented himself in a favorable light in every move he made. His enemies were always wrong, and he did not hesitate to show his hatred even for those who had died. He, of course, was always right.

The memoirs, *Gedanken und Erinnerungen* (*Reflections and Reminiscences*), were published in three volumes. The first two appeared in 1898. The third volume could not be issued with the first two, because it contained malicious chapters in which Bismarck denounced the personality, character, and reputation of William II. This third volume was not published until after the defeated William had abdicated his throne at the end of World War I and had retired to Doorn, Holland.

Bismarck's eldest son, Herbert, was a special problem for the old man fretting at Friedrichsruh. The chancellor had hoped to see his son succeed him in political office. There was deep affection between father and son. "I know of no one," said the chancellor in 1889, "who could replace Herbert. I have made him the repository of all my experience—him and nobody else." But the elder Bismarck, ordinarily an expert judge of human character, was blind to the faults of his son. Herbert, like many sons of distinguished fathers, lacked the genius of his parent.

The characters of both father and son were revealed in Herbert's marital affairs. There had been trouble in 1881 when Herbert declared his intention of marrying a princess of the Silesian aristocracy and a divorcee. The chancellor was appalled because the young lady belonged to a family which he included among his hated enemies. He used every weapon he could against the proposed marriage. He burst into rages, appealed to Herbert in the name of pity, proposed to disinherit his son, and even threatened to commit suicide. He had his way—the marriage plans were cancelled.

Herbert had to bear the burden of this for the rest of his life. People regarded him as a cad who had gone back on his word and ruined a lady's life. They called him a weakling who could not break away from his father's control. The unhappy Herbert became irritable and melancholy. Taking refuge in alcohol, he became a notorious drunkard.

When his father retired in 1890, Herbert, then forty-one, resigned his office too. Saddened, he sacrificed what had started out to be a brilliant political career. When Bismarck was asked to persuade Herbert to stay, he replied: "My son is of age!"

In 1892 Herbert, accompanied by his parents, went to Vienna to marry an Austrian lady. The journey to the Austrian capital became a kind of triumphal tour. Everywhere huge crowds turned out to honor and welcome Bismarck, the creator of united Germany. William II was concerned by this outburst of popular sentiment, which might possibly propel Bismarck back to power. The emperor ordered the German ambassador in Vienna to avoid the marriage ceremony. Bismarck was not even permitted an audience with the Austrian emperor. This was insulting treatment. The miserable quarrel had descended to a low level.

It was on this same trip to Vienna that Bismarck began to doubt the value of his life's work. He had always hated the democratic idea. He had believed it to be stupid to expect the common people to know what was good for them. There always had to be direction from above. But now, viewing with satisfaction the great crowds that came to see him, and sensing their good will and strength, he began to ask himself strange questions. Had he erred in making the power of the Crown far too great? Should he not have seen to it that the *Reichstag* have much greater power?

Those were embarrassing but vital questions. Bismarck, indeed, had failed in a critical task. When he had held the reins of government in his hands he had had the power to train his people in the ways of democracy. Instead, he had done far too much to deprive the Germans of their sense of freedom, of individual independence, of justice and humanity. In the Bismarck era the German people were cast in the solid mold of obedience. They became accustomed to the idea of accepting orders without question from the power above them. They were denied the privileges of a democratic society.

That is the key to the tragic history of Germany after Bismarck. One day the German people, accustomed to obedience, would take orders from one of the most bestial dictators in the long history of mankind—a violent little Austrian named Adolf Hitler.

CHAPTER TWENTY-FOUR

Finale

*"For me there is only one more happy day.
That is the day I shall not wake up again."*

At first Bismarck was glad to get away from Berlin. "I just don't like the stink of civilization in the big cities," he said. He enjoyed the attention of his visitors, but fewer people came as the years went by. He became restless in his solitary life with its empty days.

His wife Johanna, however, seemed to be satisfied, for she had always hated Berlin and its hectic life. She was happy to be without interminable social obligations. She had aged considerably—now she was a thin, little old woman. Weakened by asthma, she was ill and irritable. She died in 1894, after a lingering illness. She had spent a lifetime catering to her husband's whims and was always there for him when he needed her. Now that his beloved wife was gone, Bismarck was left lonely and desolate.

April 1, 1895, was Bismarck's eightieth birthday.

Princes, high officials, members of the *Reichstag*, professors, students—all came to Friedrichsruh to honor the old man. Even William II appeared. After leading several squadrons of cavalry on horseback, the emperor delivered a birthday address. Bismarck quietly acknowledged the honor but he never for a moment forgot that this was the man who had thrown him out of office.

Every once in a while the impulsive emperor, surrounded by a fawning entourage, would descend on Friedrichsruh to see the retired chancellor. Bismarck hated these unexpected visits. He was sure that William's only reason for coming was to see how much closer Bismarck had come to his grave.

In fact, the old feud flared up again. At a dinner party in 1897, Bismarck slowly and deliberately turned to the emperor and said: "Your Majesty, as long as you have this officer corps, you can, of course, permit yourself to do whatever you please. But when this is no longer the case, it will be very different." The dinner guests were appalled by this grim frankness. But William appeared to be unaffected and went on talking as if he had heard nothing.

After dinner, Bismarck, still trying to control his emotions, made another prophecy: "Twenty years after the death of Frederick the Great the battle of Jena had been fought and lost. Twenty years after my death the great crash will come if things go on as they are."

It was a remarkable prediction. Bismarck died in July, 1898; William II's Germany crashed in ruins in November, 1918.

The retired chancellor began to think more and more about his own end. Back in 1887, he had said: "Years ago I worked it out by cabalistic reckoning that I would die in 1886 at the age of seventy-one. Here it is 1887 and that has not happened. I shall, therefore, die in my eighty-third or eighty-fourth year."

Indeed, in his eighty-fourth year the signs of old age had set in on Bismarck. His hair had turned white, his steps were slow and weak, he could no longer walk through his beloved woods. The once powerful body began to decay rapidly. The terrible facial pains, from which he had suffered throughout his life, became even worse. He could not sleep. He was in obvious physical torture. In late July, 1898, came an inflammation of the lungs which exhausted him. He suffered agony from a thirst which he could not satisfy. For two days he became weaker and weaker. His doctor gave him morphine and placed hot sponges on his body.

On July 30, 1898, the family gathered around the deathbed. Bismarck's fever rose higher and higher as his heart weakened. Then came a rattling noise. It was all over. The great Bismarck was dead.

Word was flashed immediately to the emperor, who was cruising along the Norwegian coast on his yacht, and who had given strict orders to be notified when events became critical at Friedrichsruh. As soon as he learned of Bismarck's death, William ordered that his ship dock at Kiel. On August 2 the emperor's train arrived at Friedrichsruh.

Bismarck's sons, Herbert and Wilhelm, gave the monarch a formal but cold reception. The emperor laid a large wreath on the coffin, already surrounded by flowers. Then the ruling Hohenzollern, whom Bismarck had despised, hurried back to his train. The visit had lasted just half an hour.

William II suggested that Bismarck be buried in the Berlin Cathedral "beside the remains of my ancestors." Herbert Bismarck vetoed that immediately. Before he died, Bismarck had left word that he wanted to be laid to rest in a small mausoleum at Friedrichsruh. And there he was buried.

That is where the great architect of German unity lies today. It is a modest building sitting on a small rise in the midst of the trees that Bismarck loved so much.

Bismarck carried his feud with Emperor William II to his grave. On his tombstone is an inscription which he wrote himself:

A TRUE GERMAN SERVANT
OF THE
EMPEROR WILLIAM I

Chronological Summary of Principal Events in Bismarck's Life

1815   April 1—Bismarck born at Schönhausen in Brandenburg

1832   Passed examinations for University

1832–33   Student at the University of Göttingen

1833–35   Student at the University of Berlin

1835   Enters governmental service as legal examiner in Berlin

1836   Government service at Aachen (Aix-la-Chapelle)

1837   Army service in the Jaeger or Rifles, at Potsdam

1841   Lieutenant in *Landwehr* (National Guard)

1847   Elected to Prussian *Landtag* (Diet)

1848   Brings peasants to Berlin to fight the revolution

1851–58   Prussian envoy to the German *Bund* at Frankfurt

1859–62   Prussian ambassador to Russia

1862   Prussian ambassador to France

1862   Prussian minister-president and foreign minister; constitutional conflict over the budget

1864   War with Denmark over Schleswig-Holstein

1866   First attempt on Bismarck's life

1866   War with Austria

1867   The North German Confederation

1870–71   Franco-Prussian War; completion of German unity

1872   Beginning of *Kulturkampf* against Catholic Church

1873   May laws; League of the Three Emperors

1874	Second attempt on Bismarck's life
1874	The Arnim affair
1878	Law against the Socialists; the Congress of Berlin
1879	Dual Alliance with Austria-Hungary
1882	The Triple Alliance: Germany, Austria-Hungary, Italy
1885	Bismarck's seventieth birthday—idolized by the German people
1887	The Reinsurance Treaty with Russia
1888	Death of Frederick III; accession of William II
1890	Bismarck's resignation
1890–98	Retirement at Friedrichsruh
1898	July 30—Death of Bismarck

Index

Walz, Dr., 32
William I, king of Prussia and
     emperor of Germany, 32–
     36, 38–39, 51–54, 56–57,
     62–67, 72–73, 75–79, 80,
     82, 83, 85–88, 96, 102–103,
     112, 113, 118–122, 135,
     138, 148
William II, emperor of Germany,
     115, 126, 127–131, 132–

136, 139–141, 143, 146,
     147–148
Windthorst, Ludwig, 92, 133–
     134
Workers, attitude toward, 130–
     131
Workers, social security benefits
     for, 105
World War I, 110, 115, 141
Württemberg, 27